HORSE T[...]
in
ARIZONA

Revised
2nd
Edition!

by

Jan Hancock

**GOLDEN
WEST ☼
PUBLISHERS**

Cover Photos by Bob Rink Photography
Interior art and maps by author

Library of Congress Cataloging-in-Publication Data

Hancock, Jan
   Horse Trails in Arizona / by Jan Hancock
      p.   cm.
   Includes index.
   1. Trail riding — Arizona — Guidebooks. 2. Trails — Arizona
     — Guidebooks.   I. Title.
SF309.256.A6H36   1994   94-12949
798.2'3 — dc20   CIP

ISBN # 0-914846-96-5

Printed in the United States of America

2nd Printing ©1998

Golden West Publishers, Inc.
4113 N. Longview
Phoenix, Az 85014 USA
(602) 265-4392

Acknowledgements

Horses seem to bring out the best in everyone. This book on horse trails was no exception. Without fail, everyone the author contacted for information, assistance, trail directions, maps or other materials responded enthusiastically and wanted to be involved in bringing this book to fruition. To all of these very professional and responsive people and agencies, the author is deeply indebted.

There are some people that deserve special mention because of their support and encouragement in the process of writing this book. Leading this list is my trail guide with the best sense of direction imaginable, my riding companion, Larry Snead. Through rain and thunderstorms, flat tires on the horse trailer, ten-hour days in the saddle and more, Larry persevered! I have pictures too numerous to count of the backs of Larry and his horse, Whiskey, as I followed them down scores of trails, trying to capture the personality of each trail on film and cassette tape.

Arizona public land agencies were particularly invaluable in providing updated maps and trail information, and even proofreading the descriptions of the trails included in this publication. Special appreciation is extended to Jim Schmid, Pam Gluck, Eric Smith, Art Matthias, Connie Birkland, Don Hoffman, Carl Taylor, Pete Weinel, Dave Killebrew, Malcolm Hamilton, John Spehar, Brad Geeck, Duane Hinshaw, Liz Hildebrand-Crossman, Robie Pardee, Holly Van Houten, Sheri Fox, Dick Streeper, Cathy Kahlow, Bob Herring, Bill Stafford, Sally Skirball, Kelly Darnell White, Brad Orr, Lisa Ross, Bob Burnett, Don Gumeringer, Chuck Holt, Owen Martin, Kathleen Moore, Beth Puschel, Bill Cook, Jesus Luceno, Mark South, Dale Mance, Carrie Templin, Russ Orr, Walt Thole, Brian Poturalski, and others too numerous to name, for all of their extra efforts.

The photography for the book cover was provided by Bob Rink Photography, and the riders in the photographs are Scott and Sherry Snead of Paradise Valley; to all three I wish to express a special thanks for their patience, talent, and resourcefulness in obtaining that "perfect picture" after repeated shooting sessions.

To my many friends in the Las Damas women's riding group goes another special thanks for your encouragement and suggestions for trails to include in the publication, especially Nancy

Lauchner, Gerry Ballinger, Margaret Bohannan, Carolyn Corbet, Laura Ford, Sara Bollman, Caroline Shupe, Cathy Hubbard, Sydney Keller, Elizabeth Jones and numerous others who kept the momentum going!

Riding companions from southern Arizona, Linda Tuck, Sinclair "Zeke" Browning, Georgia Keefer, Rosemary Minter, Scottie Bidegain, Jan Gingold, Dean Prichard, Ken Eckle, and Curt Moore, thank you for sharing your trails with me and making me feel so welcome.

Family members provided constant support and encouragement in multiple ways to complete this book. My mother, Dr. Agnes E. "Peg" Hartnell, also an author, spent many hours researching information for this publication at the library, and many more hours proofreading the final draft. My son, Brian, helped me tremendously with my laptop computer, giving me just what I needed to know, exactly when I needed it! My horseback riding sister, Hanna, was my personal cheerleader.

Talented veterinarians contributed their time and thoughts to this publication...I'd like to thank my wonderful father, William F. Hartnell, D.V.M., for putting me on my first horse and instilling the love of riding in me forever, and for his professional contributions to the veterinarian's list in this publication, along with those of Vicki Baumler, D.V.M., of Phoenix, and Carolyn Lee, D.V.M., of Dewey, Arizona.

To my trail-wise, willing, and well-traveled horse, Partner, thanks for the good times...you made it fun.

And others, Barry Goldwater, Emery Henderson, Richard Williams, Joan Haldiman, Mike Flynn, Bev Garcia, Barbara "Bob" Wolfe, Martin Ross, Pam, Jayson and Michelle Mead, Don and Sandy Nagel, Tom Tulloh, Brookie Maxwell, Jan Alfano, Bill Lauchner, Tom Cox, Billy Brandt, Mike Cobb, Bob Nordham, Larry Snead, Jr., Mel Counseller, Jon and Marywade Gilbert, Jim and Gayle Higgs, Lee Fischer, Karin Wade, my proofreading friends and neighbors, and all who have contributed their special piece to the puzzle of writing a book on horse trails.

My sincere thank you.

Introduction

It's thrilling to experience the wonder of Arizona on horseback!

The trails in this book were selected because they have many of the features horseback riders want...good roads to the trailheads with a large space to park horse trailers; well-defined or signed trails with trail conditions suitable for horses; wilderness trails or trails restricted to non-motorized use; water available for horses near the trailhead or on the trail; and interesting trail highlights.

Arizona is unique because so much of the land in the state belongs to the people, giving equestrians a vast playground border-to-border. The many climates Arizona captures are also unique, from desert lowlands to mountaintop alpine, which adds up to a tempting variety of places to go with your horse when the weather is right...year-round.

A vast network of horse trails criss-crosses the state; some are the original trails ridden as few as 100 years ago by Arizona pioneers. There's a special inspiration, almost wonderment, as you ride a trail with trees still bearing the blaze marks of horseback explorers who rode the same path such a short time before you.

Most of the trails listed in this guide are one-day rides or less, and many of the trails were included because they were close to urban centers where busy people try to carve some time to share with their favorite horse. An effort was made to include trail systems where loop rides were possible. Trails are also included that would make a fabulous overnight, weekend, or extended horseback vacation.

Some segments of the new Arizona Trail are featured in this book. The Arizona Trail is a 780-mile non-motorized trail linking Arizona from the border of Mexico to the border of Utah.

Arizona has it all...pine and aspen forests; cool mountain summers; warm, sunny winters; gold mines; cliff dwellings; bald eagles; mountain sheep, elk, antelope and deer; wildflower carpets; ranches and cowboys; streams full of trout; chuckwagon breakfasts; and even restaurants with hitching posts...all to be enjoyed from the back of a horse!

Read on, and saddle up!

Table of Contents
(Detailed Trail Descriptions)

Map #	Trail Name	County	Page
1 —	Mount Baldy Wilderness Trails	Apache	1
2 —	Cochise Stronghold Trails	Cochise	4
3 —	General Crook Trail-Mogollon Rim Loop	Coconino	7
4 —	Jacks Canyon Trail	Coconino	10
5 —	San Francisco Peaks Trails Kachina Peaks Wilderness Trails & The Elden/Dry Lake Hills Trail System	Coconino	13
6 —	Hellsgate Wilderness Trail	Gila	17
7 —	Highline Trail See Canyon & Two-Sixty Trailheads	Gila	19
8 —	Horton Creek Loop Trails	Gila	23
9 —	Pine Trailhead	Gila/Coconino	25
10 —	Roosevelt Lake Trails /Frazier Trailhead	Gila/Pinal	27
11 —	Mount Graham Trails	Graham	30
12 —	Hannagan Meadow Trails	Greenlee	34
13 —	Alamo Lake State Park Trails	LaPaz	38
14 —	Black Canyon Trail Emery Henderson Trailhead	Maricopa	41
15 —	Cave Creek Recreation Area Trails	Maricopa	43
16 —	Dreamy Draw Trails Charles M. Christiansen & Perl Charles Trails	Maricopa	46
17 —	Estrella Mountain Regional Park Trails	Maricopa	49
18 —	Jacob's Crosscut Trail	Maricopa/Pinal	52
19 —	McDowell Mountain Regional Park Trails	Maricopa	54
20 —	Seven Springs Recreation Area Trails	Maricopa	57
21 —	South Mountain Regional Park Trails	Maricopa	60
22 —	Usery Mountain Recreation Area Trails	Maricopa/Pinal	64
23 —	White Tank Mtn. Regional Park Trails	Maricopa	67
24 —	Lake Havasu City Area Trails	Mohave	70
25 —	Pinetop/Lakeside Trails - Blue Ridge Trail	Navajo	72
26 —	Catalina State Park Trails	Pima	75
27 —	Saguaro National Park East Trails	Pima	78
28 —	Saguaro National Park West Trails	Pima	81
29 —	Tucson Mountain Regional Park Trails	Pima	85
30 —	The Arizona Trail/American Flag Trailhead	Pinal	88
31 —	Superstition Wilderness Trails	Pinal/Maricopa	92
32 —	Florida Canyon Trail	Pima/Santa Cruz	95
33 —	Juan Bautista de Anza Nat'l. Hist. Trail	Santa Cruz	98
34 —	The Arizona Trail/Canelo Pass Trailhead	Santa Cruz	101
35 —	General Crook Trail Copper Canyon	Yavapai	104
36 —	Granite Mountain Area Trails	Yavapai	107
37 —	Groom Creek Horse Camp Trails	Yavapai	110

Map #	Trail Name	County	Page

38 — Red Rock/Secret Mountain Wilderness Trails
Long Canyon & Loy Canyon Trails .... Yavapai 113
39 — West Spruce Mountain Trail .... Yavapai 118
40 — Woodchute Wilderness Trail .... Yavapai 121
41 — Yeager Canyon Loop Trails....................... Yavapai 124
42 — Kofa Queen Trail .... Yuma 127

Contact Agencies... *130*
Equipment Check Lists for Trail Riders & Horse Trailers *135*
Trail Manners, Overnight Camping and Trail Safety *138*
Hitchin' Post Restaurants & Overnight Accommodations *140*

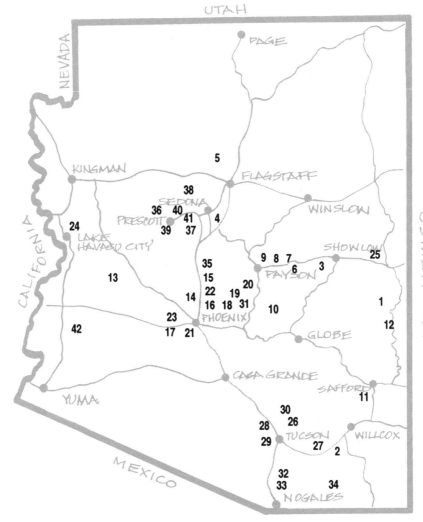

Barry Goldwater

Ms. Jan Hancock
Outdoor Adventures Unlimited
P.O. Box 33582
Phoenix, AZ   85067

Dear Jan:

Would that I could set down my favorite trail, I really
enjoyed those wonderful rides with a good horse. But I'm
afraid I can only live in memory of this, because I'm 83
now, and my most active time was before I was 20.

I would say that the trails around Iron Springs, and around
Prescott, and Granite Mountain are the ones I remember most.
The details are hard to remember, but if those trails are
still there, I would recommend them to anyone who loves
beauty, and adventure.

Sincerely,

Barry Goldwater

Author's Note:

I have dedicated the Granite Mountain Trail section (pages 107-109) to Senator Goldwater in honor of his love for Arizona and his many achievements in behalf of our state. Senator Goldwater wrote this letter to the author in 1992.

Index to All Trails Shown on Maps

Page #

Abineau #127 15
Alamo Lake 39
Apache Spring 44
Arcadia Nat'l. Rec. #328 .. 32
Arizona (Am. Flag) 89
Arizona (Canelo Hills) 102
Ash Creek #307 32
Bajada 61
Bajada Vista 79
Bear Jaw #26 15
Black Canyon 42
Black Mesa #241 93
Blevins 65
Blue Ridge #107 73
Boynton Canyon #47 115
Brookbank #2 16
Brown Mountain 86
Cabrillo 79
Catalina Equestrian 76
Canyon Loop 76
Cave Creek #4 58
Cave Creek Wash 44
Cedar Spring #41 108
Charles M. Christensen 47
Cholla 79
Clark Spring #40 108
Cochise #279 5
Cody #9 89
Cottonwood # 247 58
Crest #144 96
David Yetman 86
Derrick Spur #32 24
Derrick #33 24
Douglas Spring 79
Dutchman's #104 93
East Fork (Phelps) #95 2
Fifty-Year 76
First Water Trailhead 93
Florida Canyon #145 96
Foote Creek #76 35
Ford Canyon 68
Freight Wagon 79
Gadsden 50
Garwood 79
General Crook #300 7

Genr'l.Crook (Copper Cnyn)105
Gilbert Ray 86
Golden Gate Loop 86
Goldfield 55
Grant Creek #305 32
Grant Creek #75 35
Groom Creek # 307 111
Guiery 44
Gunsight Pass 44
Hellsgate #37 18
Highline #31 (Pine Trailhead) . 26
Highline #31 (See Canyon-
  Two-Sixty Trailheads) ... 21
Holbert 61
Horse Camp Loop 111
Horton Creek #285 24
Hugh Norris 82
Humphreys Peak #151 15
Jacks Canyon #55 11
Jacob's Crosscut #58 53
Juan Bautista de Anza 99
Kachina #150 15
Kennedy 79
King Canyon 82
Kiwanis 61
Kofa Queen 128
Lake Havasu City 71
Little Elden Springs Horse-
  camp Connector 16
Little Granite Mtn. #37 108
Little Yeager #533 125
Loma Verde 79
Long Canyon #122 115
Loy Canyon #5 115
Marijilda Creek 32
Mesquite 79
Mica View 79
Mormon 61
National #162 61
Noon Crk. Ridge #318 32
Old Baldy #372 96
Oracle Ridge #1 89
Pack Saddle Historical 50
Paradise #74 35
Pass Mountain #282 64

Pemberton 55
Perl Charles #1A 47
Pine Canyon #26 26
Pink Hill 79
Prospector 86
Quien Sabe #250 58
Rainbow Spur 50
Rainbow Valley 50
Ranger 61
Rock Knob Buggy 50
Rocky Ridge #153 16
Roosevelt Lakes 28
Round-the-Mtn. #302 32
Scenic 55
Schultz Creek #152 16
Second Water #236 93
Sendero Esperanza 82
Shake Trail #309 32
Shantz 79
Sheep Crossing 2
Skull Mesa #248 58
Skunk Tank #246 58
Squeeze Pen 79
Steeple #73 35
Stockton Pass #309 32
Stoneman Historical 55
Sun Circle (S. Mtn.) 61
Sunset #23 16
Super #134 96
Superstition Loop 65
Talc Mine 44
Three Tank 79
Upper Grant #65 35
Upper Pasture #38 108
Vista 79
Weatherford #102 15
Wentworth 79
West Fork #94 2
West Spruce Mtn. #264 .. 119
White Rock Sprg. #39 108
Wildhorse 79
Wolf Creek Loop 111
Woodchute #102 122
Yeager Cabin #111 125
Yeager Canyon #28 125

How to use this Trail Guide

LOCATION: This information gives you a brief description of where the trail is located (area of the state, highway and nearby towns).

LENGTH: Either one-way, loop, or other indication. Allow one hour for every two miles at a normal walking gait of the average trail horse.

SEASON: Best times to ride each trail. 3,500 to 4,000-foot elevations can be year-round trails. Always check weather forecasts!

USE: Rated on a scale from light, to moderate, to heavy. Scale reflects all trail users, not just equestrians.

RATING: The trails are rated on the basis of easy, moderate, difficult, and very difficult. An **easy** trail has little elevation change or rocky trail areas. A **moderate** trail will have elevation changes, some rocky areas or might offer trail challenges, such as a small stream or other natural land feature. **Difficult** trails have 500-1,000-foot elevation changes and the resulting areas of slopes, canyons etc. These trails require a horse with trail experience and good conditioning. **Very difficult** trails are only for the most experienced trail riders and horses. There may be elevation changes of 1,000 feet or more, very steep or rocky areas, some narrow trails. These ratings are only the author's interpretations of trail conditions.

ELEVATION: The range in elevation encountered on the trail is given. This is an approximate elevation, but it is a good indicator of the temperatures and weather you may encounter.

USGS MAP: U. S. Geological Survey maps. Remember, many of the USGS maps are eight or more years old, so you may find many changes.

CONTACT AGENCY: The agency that manages the public land which contains the trail is given. See Contact Agencies listed in this book.

HORSE TRAILER PARKING: Pull-through parking is one-direction parking. Turn-around parking indicates that a vehicle and 16-20 foot horse trailer can make an opposite direction turn without backing up.

WATER FOR HORSES: Water may be in a water tank or trough for livestock or wildlife, or in a stream, lake, or spring. If your horse isn't willing to drink from these water sources, be prepared to provide your own water supply. If indication is "not dependable," be sure to bring your own.

CORRALS: If you use these public facilities, bring a manure rake or shovel to clean up for the next user.

OTHER FACILITIES: If comfort stations (restrooms), lighting, or other amenities exist at the trailhead or on the trail, this information is given.

ACCESS: Travel directions are provided under this heading. Few of these trails require more than 8 miles of dirt or gravel road travel.

DESCRIPTION: Trail directions, characteristics, scenery, highlights, and conditions are given here.

PLEASE NOTE: Include an Arizona road map when planning your trip. Again, *always check weather conditions* expected at your destination.

Mount Baldy
Wilderness Trails

LOCATION: In the White Mountains, south of State Route 260 between Springerville and McNary.

LENGTH: 19 mile loop

COUNTY: Apache

USE: Moderate to Heavy

SEASON: June through Sept.

RATING: Difficult

ELEVATION: 9,200' to 10,800'

USGS TOPO MAP: Mount Baldy

CONTACT AGENCY: Apache-Sitgreaves National Forest, Springerville Ranger District

HORSE TRAILER PARKING: A camp designed exclusively for equestrian use; provides excellent pull-through parking.

WATER FOR HORSES: A pond fed by the East Fork of the Little Colorado River is located down a short slope at the end of the road into the horse camp. The trail to Mount Baldy crosses the stream as well.

CORRALS: The camp provides 5 wooden corrals tucked into the pines. If the weather has been rainy the corrals can become boggy. Some corrals are on a slight slope.

OTHER FACILITIES: Comfort station, 5 undeveloped campsites with corrals.

ACCESS: Travel east of Payson or west of Springerville on State Route 260 to State Route 273 which leads south and becomes FR 113 after 5 miles, where the road enters Apache-Sitgreaves National Forest. This road is paved for 5.8 miles, then turns into a good graveled road. Travel approximately 7 miles on the graveled road, pass Sheep Crossing, and when the road crosses a cattle guard after 11 miles, make a note of your odometer reading. Continue traveling another 1.7 miles until the road climbs a slope. A sign on the right at the top of the rise directs you to the Gabaldon Horse Campground. Go slowly approaching the turnoff (it's easy to miss because it's hidden by the hill). If the horse camp is full and all the

(Continued)

Mt. Baldy Wilderness Trails

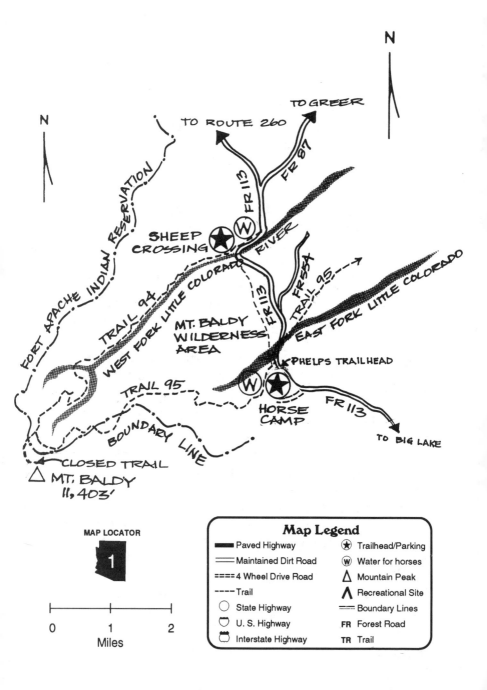

N

N

TO GREER

TO ROUTE 260

FR 113

FR 87

FORT APACHE INDIAN RESERVATION

SHEEP CROSSING

W

COLORADO RIVER

TRAIL 94

WEST FORK LITTLE COLORADO

FR 113

FR 95A

TRAIL 95

EAST FORK LITTLE COLORADO

MT. BALDY WILDERNESS AREA

PHELPS TRAILHEAD

TRAIL 95

W

HORSE CAMP

FR 113

BOUNDARY LINE

TO BIG LAKE

CLOSED TRAIL

△ MT. BALDY 11,403'

MAP LOCATOR

1

0   1   2
Miles

Map Legend

▬ Paved Highway	⊛ Trailhead/Parking
═ Maintained Dirt Road	Ⓦ Water for horses
==== 4 Wheel Drive Road	△ Mountain Peak
----- Trail	Λ Recreational Site
◯ State Highway	⋯⋯ Boundary Lines
⬡ U. S. Highway	**FR** Forest Road
⬡ Interstate Highway	**TR** Trail

corrals are in use, there is day parking only between the road and the camp. You'll have to tether your horse.

NOTE: If you plan to tether horses to trees, be certain to cushion tether ropes to avoid damage to trees and use picket lines between trees for tethering so horses won't damage tree roots.

NOTE: Additional camping with horses is available on Forest Road 409 located northeast of Gabaldon campground, or on Burro Mountain just south of Gabaldon campground.

DESCRIPTION: The trailhead to the East Fork (Phelps) Trail #95 on the southern slopes of Mount Baldy is located at the end of the road which enters the horse camp. This trail is approximately 7 miles to the half-way point around Mt. Baldy. Follow the trail to the crossing of the East Fork of the Little Colorado River, then turn left to enter the wilderness area. The trail crosses a broad, grassy area, then begins a slow, steady ascent to reveal vistas from the pine and fir trees to the streams and valleys below. Rock outcroppings and high mountain flowers add a special visual treat to equestrians all along this trail. Near the top of the mountain there will be views of major mountain ranges such as the Piñalenos, Galiuros, and Santa Catalinas.

A mile from the summit the trail meets the West Fork (Sheep Crossing) Trail #94 coming up the north side of Mt. Baldy, which is approximately 7 miles in length. It is a much rockier trail on the north side. If you continue on Trail #94 and descend Mount Baldy to the West Fork trailhead it is another 4 miles back to the horse camp (the trail is near FR 113). This route makes the entire loop around the mountain slightly over 19 miles in length. Shorter rides on portions of the trails provide rewarding views in both directions, so you don't have to ride the entire length of this trail to enjoy it.

NOTE: The summit of Mount Baldy is on the Fort Apache Indian Reservation and access is available only by special permit. Do not attempt to ride on the summit trail or cross the boundary.

The Mount Baldy Wilderness area is approximately 7,000 acres, one of the smallest in the state. To reduce the impact of heavy use, all groups using the wilderness trails are not to exceed 12 persons. The maximum number for overnight camping is 6.

Cochise Stronghold Trails

LOCATION: Approximately 50 miles east of Tucson and 27 miles south of Interstate 10 in the Dragoon Mountains.

LENGTH: 4 3/4 miles one way   **COUNTY:** Cochise

USE: Moderate   **SEASON:** Year-round

RATING: Moderate   **ELEVATION:** 5,000' to 6,000'

USGS TOPO MAP: Cochise Stronghold

CONTACT AGENCY: Coronado National Forest, Douglas Ranger District

HORSE TRAILER PARKING: Large, flat grassy area for parking horse trailers for day use only right at the trailhead. If you are staying overnight you must utilize the undeveloped camping area which has pull-through and turn-around parking. It is on the opposite side of the road just before the equestrian trailhead.

WATER FOR HORSES: No dependable water at trailhead or camping area. There is often water at Cochise Spring or Halfmoon Tank on the trail. If you bring water containers, there is water available at a spigot beside the comfort stations in the Cochise Stronghold Campground one mile from the equestrian trailhead at the end of the road. Horses are restricted from this campground area.

OTHER FACILITIES: None at the equestrian trailhead. The campground for non-equestrians has picnic tables, BBQ grills, comfort stations, and water.

ACCESS: Travel east of Tucson on Interstate 10 to Dragoon Road, (Exit 318) and travel 14 miles to U.S. Route 191. Turn south (right) and travel approximately 10.5 miles and turn west (right) near mile marker 46 on Ironwood Road to Cochise Stronghold. The paved road ends in 0.6 mile and a good, well-maintained dirt road takes you 6.8 miles to the equestrian trailhead. If you plan to camp overnight, you must use the undeveloped camping area in the oak trees on the west (right) side of the road just before the sign pointing to the equestrian trail located on the east (left) side of the road.

(Continued)

Cochise Stronghold Trails

N

FOREST ROAD 795

EQUESTRIAN CAMPING AREA

FR 281

TO HIGHWAY 191

IRON WOOD ROAD

EQUESTRIAN TRAILHEAD

STRONGHOLD DIVIDE

FR 688

HALFMOON TANK

TRAIL 279

TR 279

EQUESTRIAN CONNECTING TRAIL

W

PUBLIC CAMPGROUND (NO HORSES)

TR 281 TRAIL 277

TRAIL 532

COCHISE SPRING

FOREST ROAD 687

FR 687F

FR 345A

GORDON O's CAMP

FR 687

FOREST ROAD 687

FR 345

FOREST ROAD 345

FOREST ROAD 345

0   1/2   1
Miles

MAP LOCATOR

2

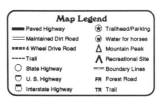

Map Legend

▬ Paved Highway	⊛ Trailhead/Parking
═ Maintained Dirt Road	Ⓦ Water for horses
▪▪▪ 4 Wheel Drive Road	Δ Mountain Peak
---- Trail	Λ Recreational Site
○ State Highway	━ Boundary Lines
▽ U. S. Highway	FR Forest Road
⬜ Interstate Highway	TR Trail

There is an uninhabited and structurally unsafe old homestead at the equestrian trailhead which is not open to the public.

DESCRIPTION: The equestrian trail is one mile long and connects with Cochise Trail #279, the main trail into the Cochise Stronghold area. This trail bypasses private property and the Cochise Stronghold Campground where horses aren't permitted.

Here in the Dragoon Mountains the Chiricahua Apache Indian leader, Cochise, signed a peace treaty with General O.O. Howard in 1872. Cochise was born in this area around 1815 and was secretly buried somewhere in the Cochise Stronghold area in 1874. Unique rock formations create dramatic backdrops for the diverse plants found here. The canyons and ridges have an abundant growth of oak, manzanita, juniper, banana yucca and bear grass.

The trails are well-maintained, have some nice areas of soft decomposed granite that is easy to ride and there are trail signs at strategic locations. There is one very difficult area just after Cochise Spring, approximately 2 miles from the trailhead. The trail steps up to go over a broad expanse of rock with a narrow cut beside a vertical rock. Be very cautious in this area (you may want to dismount and lead your horse to avoid being pinned against the vertical rock should your horse slip).

You may choose the length of your ride by selecting your destination after reaching the Cochise Trail. Cochise Spring is 1 mile, Halfmoon Tank is 2 miles, Stronghold Divide is 3 miles, and West Stronghold is 4 miles. The trail route crosses a small stream bed that flows seasonally and passes by a few cottonwood and sycamore trees. When you reach Cochise Spring there is a grassy area that makes a nice rest stop; sometimes the spring is dry. Within the next three quarters of a mile you will go through a few switchbacks and reach Halfmoon Tank. This is a catchment pond with a few cattails along its edges. At 3 miles is Stronghold Divide, the highest area on the ride, separating the east and west strongholds. If you wish to go to the end of this trail, it drops steeply into the West Stronghold and goes through many switchbacks for 1-3/4 miles until it meets a 4WD road. There are some Arizona cypress, sycamores, and walnut trees by a creek bed near the road in this area. Unless you have arranged a pick-up at the West Stronghold, it is recommended that you turn around at the divide and return to the trailhead on the same trail, enjoying the beauty of the rock formations and vistas from a totally different angle.

General Crook Trail
Mogollon Rim Loop

LOCATION: On the Mogollon Rim, between Payson and Heber, immediately south of the junction of State Route 260 and FR 300 to Woods Canyon Lake.

LENGTH: 9 mile loop

USE: Moderate

RATING: Easy

COUNTY: Coconino

SEASON: May through Nov.

ELEVATION: 6,500'

CONTACT AGENCY: Apache-Sitgreaves National Forest, Chevelon Ranger District.

USGS TOPO MAP: Woods Canyon, OW Point

HORSE TRAILER PARKING: Pull-through day parking is available at the Mogollon Rim Visitor Information Center right at the General Crook Trail information sign. This is a busy, paved parking area. Additional pull-through parking is available if you continue down the dirt road south of the Information Center on Forest Service Road 171 and pull into one of the 50 campsites.

WATER FOR HORSES: None available at trailhead. There is seasonal water in Mosquito Lake at the junction of FRs 512 and 171. Otherwise, there is water available in Christopher Creek 7 miles west of the trailhead on State Route 260. Be certain to bring water containers with you for this ride.

CORRALS: None

ACCESS: Travel on State Route 87 to Payson, and turn east on State Route 260 at the north end of town. The trailhead is located 31 miles east of Payson on Route 260. Turn south at mile marker 282.4 into the parking area for the Mogollon Rim Visitor Information Center. The General Crook Trail is marked with an information sign at the southeast corner of the parking lot.

DESCRIPTION: General George Crook and his horseback troops established this trail in the 1870's while patrolling the Arizona territory for Indians between Fort Apache and Fort Whipple. Today, even though modern roads now follow this original route, much of

(Continued)

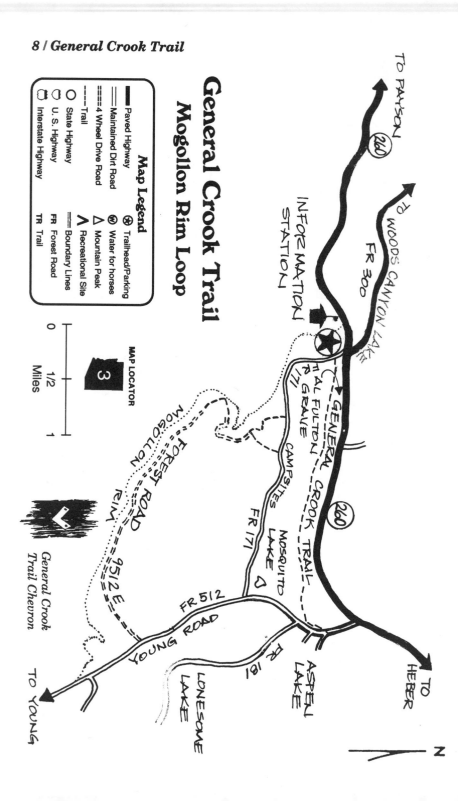

General Crook Trail
Mogollon Rim Loop

Map Legend

▬ Paved Highway	⊕ Trailhead/Parking
══ Maintained Dirt Road	⑭ Water for horses
⩵⩵ 4 Wheel Drive Road	△ Mountain Peak
----- Trail	⋀ Recreational Site
○ State Highway	⁝⁝⁝ Boundary Lines
◖ U. S. Highway	FR Forest Road
▭ Interstate Highway	TR Trail

MAP LOCATOR

3

0   1/2   1
Miles

General Crook
Trail Chevron

N

the original trail still exists and can be ridden by equestrians. Some of the old oak and ponderosa pine trees along the trail have the original blazes on them that were made to mark the trail. The trail was also the main telegraph route between the forts and a number of the white insulators that held the telegraph line can still be seen up high on the trees.

This portion of the General Crook Trail parallels Route 260 through some open, fairly flat ponderosa forest. Follow the gold and white "V" shaped chevrons to stay on the trail. In less than half a mile you will pass near the old gravesite of Al Fulton, which is 600 yards north of the General Crook Trail, marked with a Forest Service sign post. Al Fulton was a sheep rancher who died in 1888 by falling into a sink hole as he tried to save his sheep from the same fate. They were being stampeded by cattle ranchers in the area who didn't want sheep on their grazing lands.

The General Crook Trail continues for another 1.6 miles until it intersects FR512, the gravel road to Young. When you reach FR512 you can either return on the same trail for a shorter 4 mile ride round trip, or you can extend your ride to a 9 mile loop by turning south and riding in the woods beside the road to Young until you reach FR9512E, which is 2 1/2 miles south of the General Crook Trail.

Mosquito Lake, on the west side of the road to Young just before FR171, is overgrown with vegetation and hard to see, but you'll know you're there because there will be mosquitos everywhere. Bring insect repellent for yourself and your horse for this short ride. Avoid riding FR171 due to the heavy motor and all-terrain vehicle traffic using this road to access the 50 campsites that line either side of the road.

The extended ride will take you to the edge of the Mogollon Rim, which has mind-boggling views of the vast Tonto National Forest below. FR9512E follows the edge of the Rim for two miles, then abruptly runs into a finger canyon of the Rim. When you reach this point, turn right and look for the logging road that will bring you back to FR171. When you reach FR171, turn west (left) and follow FR171 back to the trailhead.

PONDEROSA PINE

Jacks Canyon Trail

LOCATION: In Sedona area, 42 miles south of Flagstaff, 11-1/2 miles east of Sedona in red rock area.

LENGTH: 4.5 miles   **COUNTY:** Coconino

USE: Moderate   **SEASON:** March through Nov.

RATING: Difficult   **ELEVATION:** 4,250' to 5,200'

USGS TOPO MAP: Munds Mountain

CONTACT AGENCY: Coconino National Forest, Sedona Ranger District

HORSE TRAILER PARKING: Ample turn-around parking by the corrals at the equestrian trailhead for Jacks Canyon Trail. (Hiker trailhead is another 1/2 mile farther on Jacks Canyon Road.)

WATER FOR HORSES: No dependable water. Water is sometimes available at Jacks Tank or in the bottom of the canyon. Water is available in Oak Creek Village or in the Sedona area.

CORRALS: None

OTHER FACILITIES: None

ACCESS: From Phoenix, drive north on Interstate 17 to Exit 298 and turn left toward Oak Creek Canyon and Sedona on State Route 179. Travel 8 miles and turn right (east) at mile post 306.2, which is the intersection of Jacks Canyon Road (FR 793). Follow this paved road for two miles, watching for a sharp right-hand turn. Look for a gate and corrals in a field to the right. Turn right at the corrals, go through the gate (close the gate if it was closed when you arrived) and park. There is a horse access gate in the fence near the corrals that leads to the trail. The access trail parallels the main road to the Pine Valley subdivision.

DESCRIPTION: This trail is in the 18,150-acre Munds Mountain Wilderness. Jacks Canyon Trail #55 follows an old 4WD road that skirts around the boundary of the subdivision for the first mile. The canyon lies between Lee Mountain on the left and Horse Mesa on the right. The canyon gains elevation as it curves north and climbs to the top of the rim on Schnebly Hill. This trail was used by ranchers to move their cattle to the top of the rim in the summer and down

(Continued)

Jacks Canyon Trail

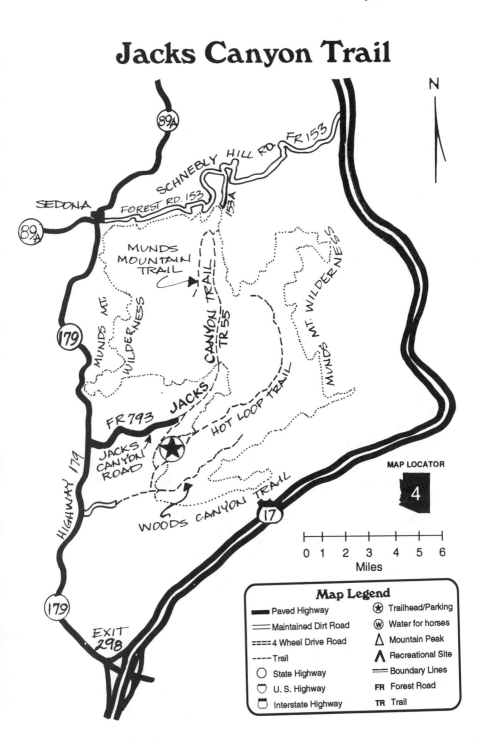

N

89A

SCHNEBLY HILL RD. FR 153

SEDONA

FOREST RD. 153

153A

89A

MUNDS
MOUNTAIN
TRAIL

MUNDS MT. WILDERNESS

179

JACKS CANYON TRAIL TR 55

MUNDS MT. WILDERNESS

FR 793 JACKS

HOT LOOP TRAIL

JACKS
CANYON
ROAD

MAP LOCATOR

4

HIGHWAY 179

WOODS CANYON TRAIL

17

179

EXIT
298

```
0  1  2  3  4  5  6
        Miles
```

Map Legend

▬ Paved Highway		✪ Trailhead/Parking	
═ Maintained Dirt Road		ⓦ Water for horses	
≡ 4 Wheel Drive Road		△ Mountain Peak	
--- Trail		∧ Recreational Site	
○ State Highway		⬌ Boundary Lines	
⬭ U. S. Highway		**FR** Forest Road	
⬔ Interstate Highway		**TR** Trail	

again to the lower elevations in the winter.

The 4WD trail goes approximately 2 miles in a northeasterly direction to Jacks Tank. After the tank you can leave the 4WD wider road and take the trail that branches off to the right toward the base of the canyon, which now begins curving northward. This is where the trail becomes very scenic, especially if there is any water running in the canyon. The erosion in the red sandstone has created interesting curvilinear patterns in the canyon walls and floor, and the canyon is quite narrow in some places.

Even though the trail continues 2 more miles to the top of the Schnebly Hill rim, it is recommended to turn around here and return to the trailhead. The trail starts to climb steeply at the 4.5 mile point and it has some dangerous, narrow sections for equestrians.

The return ride will give you some magnificent views of the Sedona red rocks that you missed when traveling in the opposite direction.

Riding up a streambed in red rock canyon country.

MAP LOCATOR

San Francisco Peaks Trails

Little Elden Spring Horse Camp Trailhead

LOCATION: 4.5 miles north of Flagstaff on U.S. Highway 89 to Page.

LENGTH: Varies with trail(s)   **COUNTY:** Coconino

USE: Moderate   **SEASON:** June through Oct.

RATING: Difficult to Very Difficult   **ELEVATION:** 7,100' to 12,000'

USGS TOPO MAP: Humphreys Peak, Flagstaff East, Flagstaff West, White Horse Hills, Sunset Crater West

CONTACT AGENCY: Coconino National Forest, Peaks Ranger District

HORSE TRAILER PARKING: All campsites and day parking areas provide ample parking with pull-through spaces. Reservations for campsites can be made by calling the Peaks Ranger District. There is a small fee per unit per day at the horse camp.

WATER FOR HORSES: Water tanker with potable water (for horses only) is provided at Little Elden Spring Horse Camp (until well and spigot are completed). Bring water bucket. Water is also available on the trail at Schultz Tank.

CORRALS: No corrals are provided at campsites or trailheads, but every campsite has two large metal hitching posts for tethering overnight. The campsite area is fully fenced.

OTHER FACILITIES: Comfort stations, picnic tables, BBQ grills, as well as rakes, wheelbarrows and shovels for manure cleanup.

ACCESS: From Phoenix travel north on Interstate 17 to Flagstaff. Take Exit 340 to Interstate 40 East (to Albuquerque) and go to Exit 201, U.S. Highway 89 to Page and the Grand Canyon. Follow the signs to Grand Canyon. Turn left to go over the freeway, then make an immediate right to go north on U.S. Highway 89. Travel 4.5 miles to FR 556, or Little Elden Spring Road. Turn left off U.S. Highway 89 on FR 556 and travel 2 miles to the horse camp entrance, which is on the north (right) side of the road.

(Continued)

If you are staying overnight, check in with the campground host on arrival. If you plan to ride the trails during the daytime only, proceed past the horse camp. At 0.8 miles ahead is a large parking turn-around for trail users and horse trailers.

The trailhead connecting to Schultz Tank, Schultz Creek, Brookbank and Sunset Trails is located just to the north of the day parking area. A connecting trail from the horse camp leads to this trailhead as well. The elevation in this trailhead area is 7,100'.

NOTE: There are 15 camp sites at Little Elden Spring Horse Camp. Some sites may be reserved by calling the Peaks Ranger District. There is a maximum stay limit of 14 days in any 30 day period to give more horse-campers opportunities to use the facilities. Firewood is not provided. Call ahead for fee and vacancy information.

DESCRIPTION: There are networks of trails to ride in the area accessed from the Little Elden Spring Horse Camp. They are either in the Kachina Peaks Wilderness, north of Schultz Tank, or the Elden/Dry Lake Hills Trail System, south of Schultz Tank.

The Kachina Peaks Wilderness trails are for hikers and equestrians, and closed to motorized vehicles and mountain bikes. The trails in the Wilderness area climb to very high elevations, so horses need to be frequently rested. The Kachina Trail #150 is particularly enjoyable, and gives some very spectacular views to trail riders. This trail is reached by riding up the Weatherford Trail. In approximately one mile you'll reach an old road that is closed to vehicles. Turn west (left) and follow this old road for approximately 0.25 mile. The Kachina Trail will intersect on the north (right) side of the trail. *There is a short area mid-way on this trail that is narrow and dangerous. Dismount and walk this area.* This trail is 5 miles in length and terminates at the Snow Bowl ski area.

Other trails in the Wilderness are: Humphreys Peak #151, (4.5 miles); Weatherford #102, (8.7 miles); Bear Jaw #26/Abineau #127, (6 mile loop); and Inner Basin #29. To protect the fragile tundra habitat, equestrians are not permitted to ride on Humphreys Peak Trail or the Weatherford Trail above Doyle Saddle. Turn around when you reach these restricted areas. Horseback riding is also prohibited on the trails in the Inner Basin, which is the source of Flagstaff's water supply.

(Continued)

Kachina Peaks Wilderness Trails

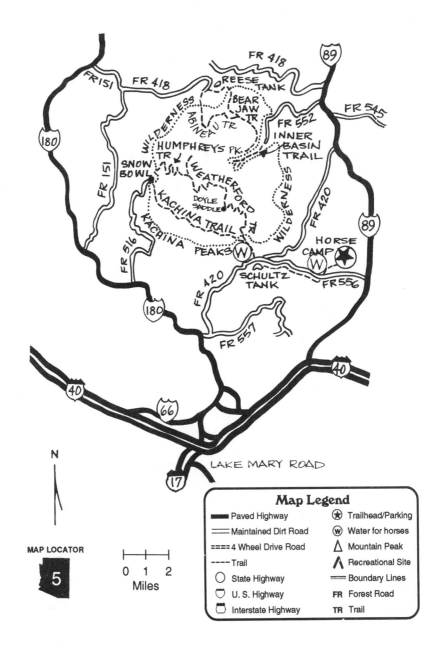

Map Legend

▬▬ Paved Highway	✪ Trailhead/Parking
═══ Maintained Dirt Road	Ⓦ Water for horses
==== 4 Wheel Drive Road	△ Mountain Peak
---- Trail	∧ Recreational Site
○ State Highway	⋯⋯ Boundary Lines
⬡ U. S. Highway	**FR** Forest Road
⬔ Interstate Highway	**TR** Trail

N

MAP LOCATOR
5

0 1 2
Miles

The Elden/Dry Lake Hills Trails System is located just south of Schultz Tank. This system offers a variety of trails: Brookbank Trail #2 (2.5 miles); Sunset Trail #23 (4 miles); Schultz Creek Trail #152 (3.5 miles); and Rocky Ridge Tail #153 (2.2 miles). *Three other trails, Fatman's Loop, Elden Lookout, and Oldam Trail from Buffalo Park to the Pipeline Trail, are closed to horseback riding.*

Mountain bikes are permitted in the Elden/Dry Lake Hills Trail System. The trails in this system pass through alternating areas of forest and meadow and provide beautiful vistas of the San Francisco Peaks and the red rock canyon country leading into the Sedona/Oak Creek Canyon area.

The Elden/Dry Lake Hills Trail System

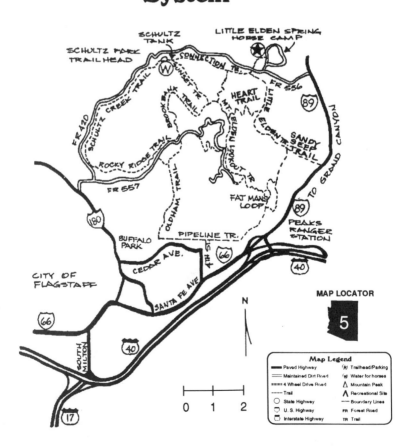

6

Hellsgate Wilderness Trail

LOCATION: East of Payson, between Star Valley and Christopher Creek.

LENGTH: 7 miles one way

USE: Light to Moderate

RATING: Moderate to Difficult

COUNTY: Gila

SEASON: April through Nov.

ELEVATION: 4,000' to 5,300'

USGS TOPO MAP: Diamond Butte, Diamond Point, McDonald Mountain

CONTACT AGENCY: Tonto National Forest, Payson Ranger Dist.

HORSE TRAILER PARKING: Pulloff with turn-around space at the trailhead on FR405A.

WATER FOR HORSES: There is a spring-fed water tank at the trailhead and a stock tank near the turn-around point on the trail, which normally has water unless there is a drought. If you bring your own water containers they can be filled at Tonto Creek, several miles east of the trailhead on State Route 260.

CORRALS: None at trailhead. Corrals and facilities for overnight camping with horses are available in Payson at Houston Mesa Horse Camp, just north of Payson off Highway 87.

OTHER FACILITIES: None at trailhead.

ACCESS: Travel to Payson on State Route 87. Turn east at the junction of State Route 260 on the north side of Payson. Travel approximately 11 miles and turn south between mile marker 262 and 263 on FR405A, just east of Little Green Valley. Travel a little less than one mile on FR 405A and turn right into the trailhead parking area. The trailhead is marked and signed for Forest Trail #37. There is a gate to the trail, at the trailhead. Head south toward the Hellsgate Wilderness Area.

DESCRIPTION: The vast and remote Hellsgate Wilderness Area between Payson and Young has some of Arizona's least explored and most pristine land. The Hellsgate Trail #37 penetrates the boundary of the wilderness area from the north, taking you just

(Continued)

above the point where Tonto Creek and Haigler Creek merge. The Hellsgate name was derived from this confluence. This is a strenuous 7 - 8 hour round-trip ride that will challenge both horse and equestrian. The trail has signage, is well-defined and has long, steep grades in some places. The distance from the trailhead to the junction of Tonto and Haigler Creek is approximately 7.5 miles, or a 3-4 hour ride. ***Equestrians are not permitted to take horses the last 1/2 mile to the creeks because of the steepness, danger, and trail damage that would be caused by horses' hooves.*** Turn around and return to the trailhead.

Hellsgate Wilderness Trail

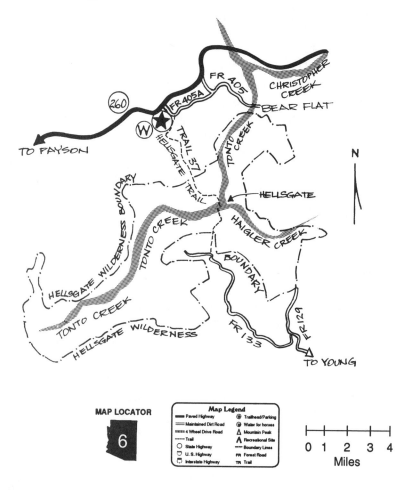

MAP LOCATOR

6

Map Legend

▬ Paved Highway	⊕ Trailhead/Parking
═ Maintained Dirt Road	⊚ Water for horses
▦ 4 Wheel Drive Road	△ Mountain Peak
---- Trail	▲ Recreational Site
○ State Highway	▬ Boundary Lines
◌ U. S. Highway	FR Forest Road
▢ Interstate Highway	TR Trail

0 1 2 3 4
Miles

Highline Trail

See Canyon Trailhead

LOCATION: East of Payson near Christopher Creek off State Route 260.

LENGTH: 6 or 7 miles one way   **COUNTY:** Gila

USE: Moderate   **SEASON:** April through Oct.

RATING: Moderate to Difficult   **ELEVATION:** 6,100' to 6,500'

USGS TOPO MAP: Promontory Butte

CONTACT AGENCY: Tonto National Forest, Payson Ranger District.

HORSE TRAILER PARKING: Ample pull-through parking at See Canyon Trailhead parking lot, 300 yards north of the trail crossing.

WATER FOR HORSES: Christopher Creek runs year-round, and it is just east of the parking lot down in the ravine.

CORRALS: Two wooden corrals, each large enough for two horses if necessary, but best with one horse in each.

OTHER FACILITIES: Comfort stations and picnic tables.

ACCESS: Travel east of Payson 22 miles on State Route 260 and turn north on Forest Service Road 284 across from the service station and store in Christopher Creek. Proceed 2 miles to the Highline Trail hiker sign, then go 300 yards north of the trail crossing to the large circle for parking at the end of the road. Overnight camping with horses is permitted at the trailhead.

DESCRIPTION: From this trailhead horseback riders can choose to go either east or west on the Highline Trail #31. If you go east, the trail crosses Christopher Creek just two minutes down the trail, then continues on toward the Two-Sixty Trailhead, which is the eastern end of the Highline Trail, 6.3 miles from the See Canyon Trailhead. The trail is marked with diamond-shaped markers nailed on the trees.

Several hundred yards after crossing Christopher Creek, the See Canyon Trail intersects the Highline Trail from the north. The See Canyon Trail is very washed out in some places. It climbs to

(Continued)

the top of the rim over very rugged terrain and is not recommended for equestrians.

If riders select the trail heading west at the trailhead, after 3 miles the trail becomes very primitive with downed trees and other barriers. This trail connects to Horton Creek Trail in 7 miles and continues on 3 more miles to reach Tonto Creek. This trail climbs very quickly from the trailhead, but soon levels off and meanders through very picturesque forests with views of the Mogollon Rim and red rock bluffs in the second mile. The ride back to the trailhead provides very different views. It is common to see elk, deer, and wild turkey along this section of the trail.

MAP LOCATOR

Highline Trail
Two-Sixty Trailhead

LOCATION: Between Payson and Heber just below the Mogollon Rim on State Route 260.

LENGTH: 6.3 miles one way **COUNTY:** Gila

USE: Moderate **SEASON:** May through Nov.

RATING: Easy to Moderate **ELEVATION:** 6,000'

USGS TOPO MAP: Promontory Butte (trail is not shown east of See Canyon) and Woods Canyon SW

CONTACT AGENCY: Tonto National Forest, Payson Ranger District

HORSE TRAILER PARKING: Ample pull-through parking in a large, open gravel parking lot.

WATER FOR HORSES: None at trailhead. Closest water to haul is at Christopher Creek, 5 miles west of the trailhead on State Route 260.

CORRALS: Two wooden corrals constructed by Arizona State Horsemen's Association are provided for public use, on a first-come/first-served basis.

OTHER FACILITIES: Comfort station at trailhead.

ACCESS: Travel 27 miles east of Payson on State Route 260. Turn north (left) on the gravel road at mile marker 278.8, and go

(Continued)

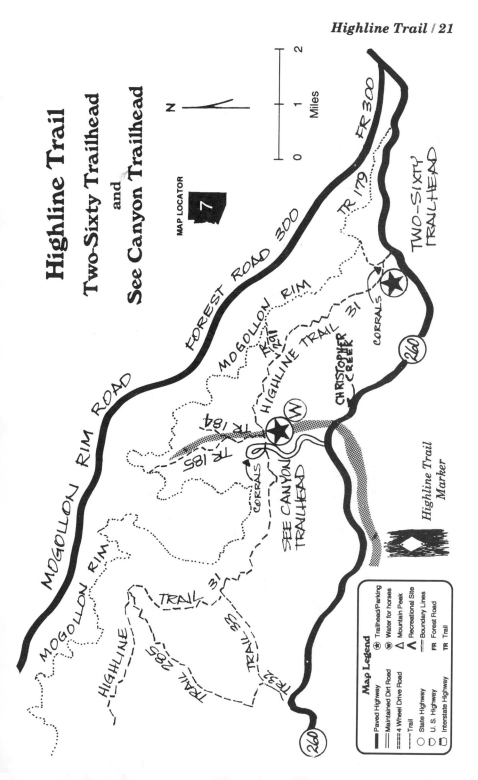

Highline Trail
Two-Sixty Trailhead
and
See Canyon Trailhead

MAP LOCATOR

7

N

Miles
0   1   2

FOREST ROAD 300

MOGOLLON RIM ROAD

MOGOLLON RIM

MOGOLLON RIM

FR 300

TR 179

TWO-SIXTY TRAILHEAD

260

CORRALS

HIGHLINE TRAIL 31

CHRISTOPHER CREEK

TR 291

TR 184

TR 185

CORRALS

SEE CANYON TRAILHEAD

HIGHLINE

TRAIL 31

TRAIL 31

TRAIL 285

TR 332

260

Highline Trail Marker

Map Legend

▬ Paved Highway	✸ Trailhead/Parking
═ Maintained Dirt Road	Ⓦ Water for horses
≡ 4 Wheel Drive Road	△ Mountain Peak
⋯ Trail	𐤠 Recreational Site
○ State Highway	‒‒‒ Boundary Lines
◑ U.S. Highway	FR Forest Road
▣ Interstate Highway	TR Trail

several hundred yards to the large parking lot on the left. Overnight camping is permitted.

DESCRIPTION: The Two-Sixty Trailhead is at the eastern end of Highline Trail #31, a 51-mile trail that winds its way through the pine forests above and below the Mogollon Rim.

The Highline Trail begins at the horse corrals at the west end of the parking area near the public restroom. The trail is well-marked with diamond-shaped markers nailed to the trees. It goes west toward the next trailhead at See Canyon, 6.3 miles away, a leisurely 3-hour ride.

The trail to See Canyon Trailhead is very scenic, meandering its way through ponderosa and oak forests while providing excellent vistas of the Mogollon Rim. The trail goes up and down into ravines, but is not exceptionally steep or difficult. Many areas are smooth, pine needle-covered paths that add to the relaxation of horse and rider. In October, the fall colors are beautiful.

Trail #179, Military Sink Hole Trail, also starts at the trailhead by the horse corrals. It goes north to connect to the General Crook Trail 2 miles away on top of the Mogollon Rim. *This trail is very steep and is not recommended for equestrians.*

Taking in the beauty of the vast Tonto National Forest from below the Mogollon Rim.

Horton Creek Loop Trails

LOCATION: Approximately 18 miles east of Payson between Star Valley and Christopher Creek on State Route 260.

LENGTH: 9.8 mile loop   **COUNTY:** Gila

USE: Heavy   **SEASON:** April through Oct.

RATING: Moderate to Difficult   **ELEVATION:** 5,700' to 6,600'

USGS TOPO MAPS: Promontory Butte (map doesn't show all trails).

CONTACT AGENCY: Tonto National Forest, Payson Ranger Dist.

HORSE TRAILER PARKING: Adequate pull-through or turn-around space in the trailhead parking lot if not full of other vehicles.

WATER FOR HORSES: Horton Creek, which begins 1/2 mile north of the trailhead, flows year-round.

CORRALS: None available. Horses may be boarded overnight at Nichol's Green Valley Ranch, 8 miles from the trailhead toward Payson. Call ahead for reservations (602-478-4493).

OTHER FACILITIES: Comfort stations, picnic tables and BBQ grills in campsites. Horses are not permitted in campsites.

ACCESS: Travel approximately 14 miles east of Payson on State Highway 260 to mile marker 268, just beyond Kohl's Ranch resort. Turn northwest (left) on FR 289 which goes to the former site of Zane Grey's Cabin and the Tonto Fish Hatchery. Drive 0.6 mile to the parking lot on the left before the bridge and Upper Tonto Creek Campground. Lead your horse to the trailhead (a right turn on the dirt road into the campground.) Trailhead is at the top of the hill.

DESCRIPTION: From the Forest Service signage and sign-in notebook, the trail immediately drops and crosses the Horton Creek stream bed, which is dry (the creek is underground here). Follow the creek on the left side and climb toward the spring where Horton Creek begins. You will be passing through rich riparian vegetation and by many small waterfalls.

When you reach Highline Trail, you have the option of returning on the same trail or heading east on Highline Trail #31 to the Derrick Trail, an additional 3.3 miles, then turning south on Derrick Trail #33 for another 2.5 miles to complete the 9.8 mile loop back to the trailhead. This loop is an all-day ride of 6-7 hours through scenic ponderosa forests with magnificent views of the Mogollon Rim. *CAUTION: Highline Trail #31 and Derrick Trail #33 back to the trailhead are very primitive. Some portions are very narrow, steep or may even be washed out. There are often downed trees or other barriers.*

Horton Creek Loop Trails

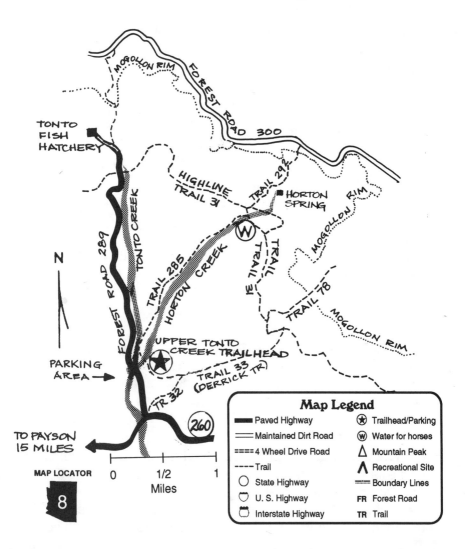

Map Legend

■■ Paved Highway	⊛ Trailhead/Parking
══ Maintained Dirt Road	ⓦ Water for horses
==== 4 Wheel Drive Road	△ Mountain Peak
---- Trail	∧ Recreational Site
○ State Highway	═══ Boundary Lines
♡ U. S. Highway	**FR** Forest Road
⬠ Interstate Highway	**TR** Trail

MAP LOCATOR

8

0   1/2   1
Miles

9

Pine Trailhead

LOCATION: Approximately 15 miles north of Payson on State Route 87 to Pine and Strawberry, west of Milk Ranch Point on the Mogollon Rim.

LENGTH: Varies with trail(s)   **COUNTY:** Gila/Coconino

USE: Light to moderate   **SEASON:** May through Oct.

RATING: Moderate to Difficult   **ELEVATION:** 5,000' to 6,000'

USGS TOPO MAP: Pine, Buckhead Mesa

CONTACT AGENCY: Tonto National Forest, Payson Ranger District

HORSE TRAILER PARKING: A large parking area with plenty of room for many trailers. Turn-around parking is available immediately off the paved highway.

WATER FOR HORSES: A man-made water tank that may have water in it is located behind the horse corrals immediately south of the fence and gate at the beginning of the trail.

CORRALS: Two wooden corrals large enough for two horses each are provided for public use at the trailhead. Arrive early, as the corrals are available on a first-come, first-serve basis.

ACCESS: From Phoenix travel to Payson on State Route 87. Continue north on Route 87 approximately 16 miles toward Pine and Strawberry. The trailhead is indicated by a sign on the east side of the highway just after mile marker 266. Drive several hundred yards down the gravel road to the parking area at the end.

DESCRIPTION: The trailhead is appealing because it has water for horses, corrals, and a restroom. The trails are fine in the area around the trailhead, but they become rocky and steep several miles away. Two trails head in opposite directions shortly after the trailhead gate. The Pine Canyon Trail #26 goes left and ends in 7.2 miles at the Upper Pine Canyon Trailhead. This is such a steep climb it would be best to turn around before going all the way to the top of the Mogollon Rim. The Highline Trail #31 is on the right. It goes through some attractive ponderosa pines and then circles around Milk Ranch Point at the 7,000' elevation range. These trails need maintenance work because rains have washed them out in many areas, leaving exposed rocks that detract from the riding pleasure they might otherwise offer.

The Pine Trailhead is located at the west end of the 51-mile Highline Trail that follows the Mogollon Rim and ends at the Two-Sixty Trailhead past Christopher Creek just off State Route 260.

Across the paved road, State Route 87, is the Oak Spring Trail #16, a 3-mile trail dropping down 400 feet to Oak Spring in a beautiful setting at the bottom of the canyon. This trail can become very muddy in certain areas near the top after a rainstorm. The Oak Spring Trail and Highline Trail are part of the Arizona Trail.

Pine Trailhead

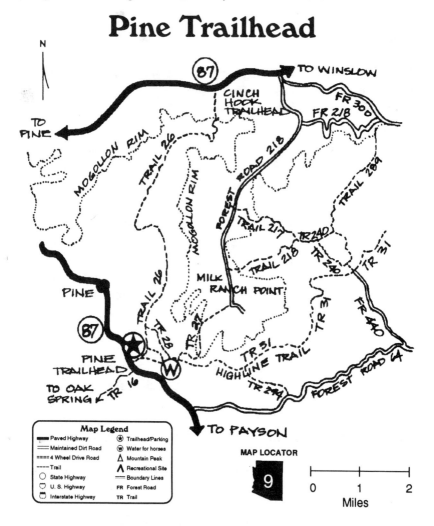

Map Legend

Paved Highway	⊛	Trailhead/Parking
Maintained Dirt Road	Ⓦ	Water for horses
4 Wheel Drive Road	Λ	Mountain Peak
Trail	Λ	Recreational Site
○ State Highway		Boundary Lines
▽ U. S. Highway	FR	Forest Road
▭ Interstate Highway	TR	Trail

MAP LOCATOR

9

0   1   2
Miles

Roosevelt Lake Trails

Frazier Trailhead

LOCATION: Northeast of Phoenix off State Route 87 to Payson on State Route 188, or northwest of Globe off U.S. Highway 60 to Miami/Globe, on State Route 88. On the south side of Roosevelt Lake near Roosevelt Dam.

LENGTH: 10-mile loop

COUNTY: Gila

USE: Light

SEASON: Sept. through May

RATING: Moderate to Difficult

ELEVATION: 2,200' to 3,400'

USGS TOPO MAP: Theodore Roosevelt Dam

CONTACT AGENCY: Tonto National Forest, Tonto Basin Ranger District

HORSE TRAILER PARKING: Large pull-through circular horse trailer parking area at trailhead.

WATER FOR HORSES: There is a water trough in the corrals at the trailhead. The trail crosses Cottonwood Creek several times and passes three springs with concrete watering troughs with floats maintained by the ranchers using the grazing rights in the area. All are available to the public through agreement with the Tonto National Forest.

CORRALS: Two wooden corrals used as holding pens, with a loading chute, are available for public use year round, except during cattle roundup season. Check with ranger district for availability.

OTHER FACILITIES: None at trailhead. There are plans for an equestrian campground under development.

ACCESS: From north or west Phoenix area, travel north on State Route 87 toward Payson (past Sunflower) to mile marker 228.3 and turn east (right) on State Route 188 to Roosevelt Lake. Travel 53 miles, going through Punkin Center, and cross the arched bridge by Roosevelt Dam. State Route 188 ends at mile marker 276.7 where it meets State Route 88. Continue on Route 88 past the Roosevelt Lake View Trailer Park and turn south (right) at the road into the Frazier electrical generating station near mile marker 243. The road

(Continued)

Roosevelt Lake Trails

Frazier Trailhead

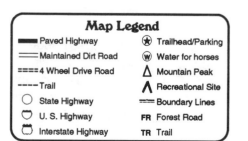

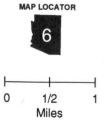

Map Legend

▬▬▬ Paved Highway	⊛ Trailhead/Parking
═══ Maintained Dirt Road	ⓦ Water for horses
==== 4 Wheel Drive Road	△ Mountain Peak
----- Trail	⋀ Recreational Site
◯ State Highway	▭▭▭ Boundary Lines
▽ U. S. Highway	**FR** Forest Road
⬠ Interstate Highway	**TR** Trail

MAP LOCATOR

6

0   1/2   1
Miles

makes a sharp right turn as you approach the substation. The trailhead is immediately off the paved highway only several hundred yards away.

From east Phoenix area, travel east on U.S. Highway 60 toward Globe, and turn north (left) at mile marker 247 on State Highway 88 to Roosevelt Lake. Travel 30 miles to Frazier trailhead, just past Tonto National Monument, on the south (left) side of the paved road.

DESCRIPTION: This scenic route takes you in a circular loop utilizing little-used four-wheel drive roads along Alchesay Canyon, around Deer Hill, and into Cottonwood Canyon, providing majestic views of the eastern slopes of Four Peaks, the Mazatzal and Sierra Ancha Wilderness areas, and an eagle's view of Roosevelt Lake.

The canyons are home to towering cottonwood trees, magnificent in November with golden yellow leaves and some of the tallest saguaro cacti in the Tonto National Forest.

The Arizona Trail from Mexico to Utah forms part of this loop trail. It continues toward the lake, crosses Roosevelt Dam and continues northward. Portions of the Arizona Trail are still under development.

Start your loop ride at Lower Cottonwood Trail #120, which is the connecting trail that leaves Frazier trailhead at the south side of the parking area and connects to the Arizona Trail one mile from the trailhead. There is an Arizona Trail sign beside Cottonwood Creek. This is the beginning of the circular loop ride around Deer Hill. Travel counter-clockwise on the route, turning right and heading downhill, crossing the stream and starting the climb out of the canyon on FR 341 (which is a section of the Arizona Trail). When you reach FR 1080, leave the Arizona Trail and turn left (south) on FR 1080, gaining elevation as you continue, then turn left (east) again on FR 341, and follow FR 341 down into Cottonwood Canyon and back to the connecting trail to Frazier trailhead. Follow the map to make the loop ride, as there is minimal signage on these trails. NOTE: You will be linking up with the Arizona Trail again as you begin your descent into Cottonwood Canyon.

. Prickly Pear

Mount Graham Trails

LOCATION: Southeastern Arizona, east of Globe/Miami and south of Safford.

LENGTH: Varies with trail(s)   **COUNTY:** Graham

USE: Light   **SEASON:** Mar.-Apr./Oct.-Nov.

RATING: Difficult to Very Difficult **ELEVATION:** 5,200' to 9,900'

USGS TOPO MAP: Mt. Graham, Webb Peak

CONTACT AGENCY: Coronado National Forest, Safford Ranger District

HORSE TRAILER PARKING: The trailheads with corrals have very well planned pull-throughs and turn-arounds that make life easy for equestrians. There are many wide pulloffs along the paved Swift Trail that skirts the top of Mount Graham, providing temporary horse trailer parking so that you can enjoy the view.

WATER FOR HORSES: Two trailheads on Mount Graham have watering troughs with spigots. The first is Round-the-Mountain Trailhead, at a lower elevation and the second is Columbine Trailhead, on top of the mountain. Water is also available at Shannon, Treasure Park, and Hospital Flat campgrounds and at the Columbine Visitor Center. Bring your own buckets as horses are not allowed in campground areas. Riggs Flat Lake on top of the mountain provides access to water for horses.

CORRALS: There are very nicely constructed pipe corrals at four locations on Mt. Graham, inviting horseback riders to linger and enjoy this rugged, remote, and lightly used area. There are 3 corrals at Round-the-Mountain Trailhead, 6 corrals at Columbine Trailhead, 4 corrals at Cunningham Trailhead, and 3 corrals at Clark Peak Trailhead, which is 3.5 miles from the end of the road on top of the mountain.

OTHER FACILITIES: The trailheads mentioned here have comfort stations, picnic tables, and most have BBQ grills or fire rings. Most equestrian campsites have a pull-through for horse trailers with individual picnic tables and BBQ grills.

ACCESS: From Tucson, travel east on Interstate 10 past Willcox and take Exit 352 to Safford on U.S. Highway 191 (formerly Hwy. 666). Travel north to mile marker 113.6, where State Route 366 turns west (left). This is the Swift Trail, a 29-mile road that is paved all the way to Heliograph Peak near the top of the mountain. From this point the road has a well-maintained gravel surface to Riggs Flat Lake and the last trailhead at Clark Peak. Allow four hours to travel from Tucson to the top of Mount Graham.

From Phoenix, travel east on the Superstition Freeway, U.S. Highway 60, toward Globe. In Globe continue east to Safford on U.S. Highway 70. As you travel through Safford, prepare to make a turn south (right) at mile marker 339.4 on U.S. Highway 191. Travel south 8 miles to the junction of State Route 366 at mile marker 113.6. Turn west (right) and proceed on the Swift Trail to the top of the mountain. Allow five to six hours to travel from Phoenix to the top of Mount Graham. Swift Trail has some long, steep grades requiring good horsepower!

DESCRIPTION: Mount Graham is one of the most rugged, wild mountains in Arizona. It has miles of trails suitable for equestrians, and offers a cool summer retreat for urban desert equestrians. *The high elevations require horses in top physical condition as many of the trails are rocky and challenging in sections. Only very experienced trail horses and riders should attempt them.*

Remember too that these elevations are subject to both snow and rainfall. Barriers such as fallen trees and washed out trails are common.

Round-the-Mountain Trailhead, just after mile marker 121, is located around the bend from a dirt road on the west (left) to Angle Orchard and Lady Bug Saddle. The trailhead is immediately to the right. The elevation is 5,200 feet. Marijilda Creek Trail (2.5 miles) and Noon Creek Ridge Trail #318 are accessed here. This is also the trailhead for the strenuous Round-the-Mountain Trail #302 that terminates at Columbine Trailhead on top of the mountain (this trail is 17 miles one way).

The Cunningham Trailhead was named after nearby Cunningham Creek. It is at 8,800 feet, approximately 19 miles from Round-the-Mountain Trailhead. There is no water at this trailhead. Grant Creek Trail #305 leads south down an old roadbed to Fort Grant 5 miles away. A loop can be made by returning on the Goudy

(Continued)

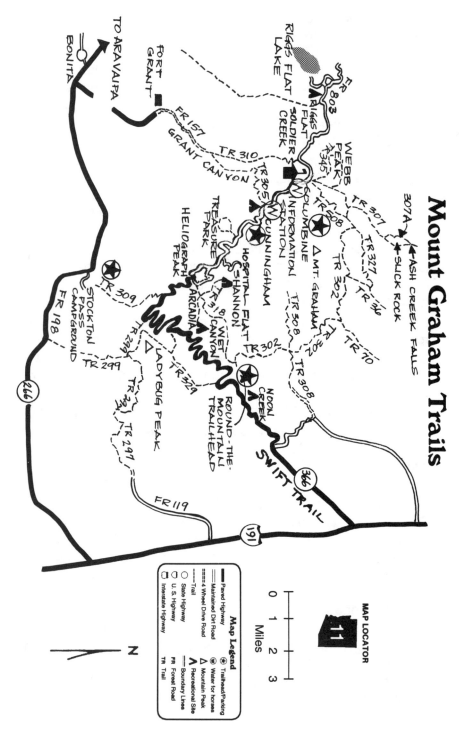

Mount Graham Trails

TO ARAVAIPA

BONITA

FORT GRANT

RIGGS FLAT LAKE

FR 803
R1665
R1665

SOLDIER CREEK FLAT

WEBB PEAK

FR 157

TR 310

GRANT CANYON

TR 305

COLUMBINE

TR 345
TR 307

INFORMATION STATION

TR 307

TREASURE PARK

CUNNINGHAM

MT. GRAHAM

TR 508

ASH CREEK FALLS

307A

SLICK ROCK

TR 327

HELIOGRAPH PEAK

HOSPITAL FLAT

TR 302

TR 36

TR 308

TR 202

TR 710

TR 309

STOCKTON PASS CAMPGROUND

SHANNON

TR 318

WET CANYON

ARCADIA

TR 302

TR 308

FR 198

TR 299

LADYBUG PEAK

TR 324

TR 331

TR 291

ROUND-THE-MOUNTAIN TRAILHEAD

NOON CREEK

SWIFT TRAIL

266

FR 119

366

191

MAP LOCATOR
11

0 1 2 3
Miles

N

Map Legend

▬▬ Paved Highway	⊛ Trailhead/Parking
═══ Maintained Dirt Road	⊛ Water for horses
≡≡≡ 4 Wheel Drive Road	△ Mountain Peak
- - - Trail	▲ Recreational Site
◯ State Highway	⌁ Boundary Lines
◯ U.S. Highway	FR Forest Road
◻ Interstate Highway	TR Trail

Canyon Trail #310, which intersects Grant Creek Trail from the west. This return route will bring you into Soldier Creek Campground, several miles west of Cunningham Trailhead. You can water your horse at Columbine Trailhead and ride beside the road back to Cunningham.

Columbine Trailhead is at an elevation of 9,520 feet and has the most attractive facilities for equestrians. There are six corrals here. The campsites are ringed with white fir, ponderosa pine, Douglas fir, aspen, Englemann spruce, Limber pine, and corkbark fir. The floor of the forest is blanketed with ferns. From this trailhead you can ride the Ash Creek Trail #307 down to the old Mount Graham sawmill site, approximately 1 mile, and continue on to Ash Creek Falls, another mile. *There is one very bad area for horses, Slick Rock, on the Ash Creek Trail. Avoid this area by taking the 307A detour.*

Round-the-Mountain Trail #302 also ends at the Columbine Trailhead so you can ride this trail for any distance you may choose. Another short trail from the Columbine corrals is the Webb Peak Trail #345. This is a 1.0 mile loop to the Webb Peak Lookout. The trail going to the right just before you reach the tower joins the Ash Creek Trail #307 at 1.7 miles.

The Clark Peak Trailhead is 5 miles beyond Columbine on a gravel road. There are three corrals, picnic tables and comfort stations, but no water. You can ride to Riggs Flat lake to water your horse. There is a sweeping view from Clark Peak Trailhead of the rugged Nuttall Canyon and the Gila River Valley. The elevation at this trailhead is 8,900 feet.

The Arcadia National Recreational Trail #38 connects the Arcadia Campground to the Shannon Park Campground. This trail is 5.1 miles in length and climbs from 6,600 feet to 9,000 feet, utilizing a lot of switchbacks to gain elevation. Access this trail at the group site area just around the curve above the entrance to Arcadia Campground. You will need a shuttle here as there is no room for trailer parking.

The trailhead for Shake Trail #309 is at the base of Mount Graham on its southern side. The equestrian trailhead is just outside of the fence surrounding the recreational area. Shake Trail is a very scenic 5.1-mile uphill ride ending at the Swift Trail on top of Mount Graham. This trailhead is an easier and closer access to Mount Graham for those traveling from the southern areas of Arizona.

MAP LOCATOR

Hannagan Meadow Trails

LOCATION: In eastern Arizona, 100 miles north of Clifton/Morenci and 22 miles south of Alpine on U.S. Highway 191 (old Highway 666).

LENGTH: Varies with trail(s)   **COUNTY:** Greenlee

USE: Light to Moderate   **SEASON:** May through Oct.

RATING: Mod. to Very Difficult   **ELEVATION:** 5,500' to 9,200'

USGS TOPO MAP: Hannagan Meadow, Strayhorse, Bear Mountain, Beaverhead.

CONTACT AGENCY: Apache-Sitgreaves National Forest, Alpine Ranger District.

HORSE TRAILER PARKING: Excellent trailhead with large turn-around gravel circle drive and ample parking.

WATER FOR HORSES: None at trailhead. Water available 4.7 miles south of trailhead off U.S. Highway 191 at K.P. Cienega campground (turn east between mile marker 226 and 227). Follow good gravel road 1.6 miles off highway into campground. A spring-fed water spigot is located near the restrooms in the campground. Fill water containers here, but do not water horses.

CORRALS: Two pipe corrals, provided by U.S. Forest Service for public recreational use. Corrals cannot be reserved, so plan an early arrival.

OTHER FACILITIES: Comfort stations.

ACCESS: From Phoenix, take U.S. Highway 60 to Globe. At a traffic light intersection in Globe (at mile marker 252.2) U.S. Highway 60 turns north to go through the Salt River Canyon to Show Low. In Show Low you can either stay on U.S. Highway 60 and continue on to Springerville, or turn south (right) at mile marker 341.6 on State Route 260 to Pinetop and continue to Springerville. When you reach Springerville, turn south on Highway 191 to Alpine (25 miles) and continue south to Hannagan Meadow (22 miles). The trailhead with corrals is located between mile markers 230 and

(Continued)

Hannagan Meadow Trails

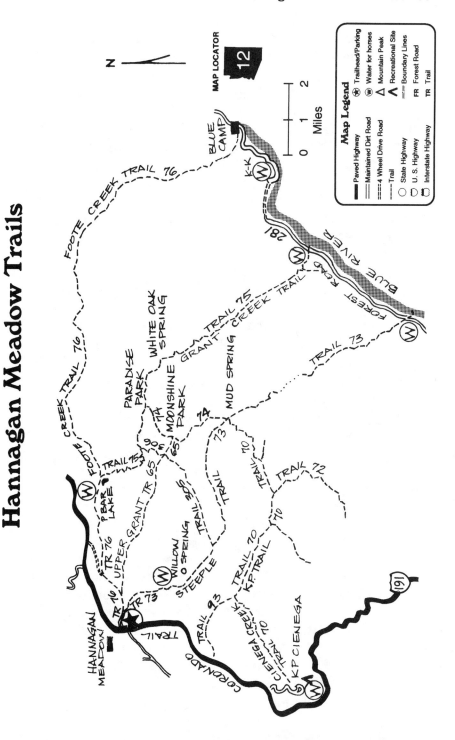

229, on the east (left) side of the highway, just beyond Hannagan Meadow Lodge. Go to the end of the gravel road (0.2 mile) where a circle turn-around, horse corrals, and comfort stations are located.

From Tucson, take Interstate 10 to U.S. Highway 191 (old Highway 666), beyond Willcox, to Safford. Turn east (right) on Highway 70 at Safford and turn north (left) on U.S. Highway 191 to Clifton/ Morenci. *You can choose two routes at a junction just after crossing the Gila River Bridge. Both have long, steep grades requiring good horsepower!*

If you select State Route 78, go to Mule Creek in New Mexico, then take U.S. Highway 180 to Luna and Alpine, and turn south on U.S. Highway 191 (old Highway 666) at Alpine and travel 22 miles to the Hannagan Meadow Trailhead. An alternate route which is shorter, but very difficult due to the extreme number of switchbacks and very slow speeds, is to turn north (left) on U.S. Highway 191 to Clifton/ Morenci and continue north to Hannagan Meadow Trailhead between mile markers 229 and 230. Turn east (right) to the trailhead, and go 0.2 mile to the parking area at the end of the road.

DESCRIPTION: Two excellent trails start at the Hannagan Meadow trailhead, and if time permits, you will want to experience both trails.

Steeple Trail #73, *an extremely strenuous overnight trip* is 13.2 miles in length. Elevations range from 5280 feet to 9200 feet, and estimated riding time is 8 hours one way. The trail winds its way through a true wilderness area rich with deep forests and cienegas (meadows). The trail is easy to follow, and there is water at Willow Spring for your horse 1.5 miles into the trail. The spring is in an open meadow, rising out of a large open metal culvert close to ground level. If you continue past Willow Spring, proceed on the Steeple Trail and toward the top of the hill a trail will cut off to the right that goes to K.P. Rim and Highway 191. For a fantastic view of the Blue River Wilderness, take this trail a few hundred yards to the edge of the rim, then return to Trail 73 toward Steeple Creek. The trail starts to become very steep and rocky at approximately 2.5 miles. You may want to turn around at this point, unless you have a very trail-wise mount. This trail reaches an intersection with Trail #74, to Moonshine Park and Paradise Park, or, if you continue on Trail #73, it goes on to Mud Spring and ends at the Blue River.

Foote Creek Trail #76 turns to the right off the main trail several hundred yards from the trailhead. This is a well-marked, newer trail which will take you on a delightful 3-mile ride through primitive forest scenery of aspens, fir, and spruce to P Bar Lake. At P Bar Lake the trail splits. Grant Trail #75 forks to the right across the meadow and starts a long descent on a very rough and rocky trail. You will be scraping your knees against the trees most of the way down the ridge. Grant Trail goes to Paradise Park and then to the Blue River, for a total distance of 10 miles from the Hannagan Meadow Trailhead.

Foote Creek Trail #76 continues on the left at P Bar Lake and descends to Foote Creek and the Blue River. This is an arduous, rocky, very difficult trail descending over 3,000 feet, 16 miles one way (9 hours). *Only the most experienced, well-conditioned horses should be used on this trail and the altitude and trail conditions warrant extreme caution against over-exertion of both horse and rider.*

Use caution when watering your horse along Foote Creek, as the poisonous water hemlock is abundant here.

Poison Hemlock

If you want to experience only the higher elevations, or prefer a good trail to build up your horse's endurance, a long loop starting at the Hannagan Meadow Trailhead and using Steeple Trail #73, Paradise Trail #74, and a portion of Grant Creek Trail #75 would connect you to Foote Creek Trail #76. This is a 9-10 hour loop.

It should be noted that the U.S. Forest Service does not recommend Trail #65 (Upper Grant Trail) or Trail #305 (Long Cienega Trail) for equestrians. Boggy ground and creek bottoms with many rocks predominate these two trails. Horses could injure themselves and/or the terrain. Moonshine Park Trail #74 is also very boggy and should be avoided.

Whichever trail you choose, you will find the truest sense of being one with nature in this natural paradise. These trails are located in the Blue Range Primitive Area where only footprints and hoofprints are allowed.

Alamo Lake State Park Trails

LOCATION: Northwest of Phoenix between Wickenburg and Quartzsite, north of Wenden on Alamo Dam Road.

LENGTH: 8 miles round trip   **COUNTY:** LaPaz

USE: Light to Moderate   **SEASON:** Oct. through April

RATING: Moderate   **ELEVATION:** 1,200' to 1,800'

USGS TOPO MAP: Alamo Dam

CONTACT AGENCY: Arizona State Parks, Alamo Lake State Park

HORSE TRAILER PARKING: Ample pull-through and turn-around parking available in equestrian campground area, with many camp-sites available. Gravel surfaced.

WATER FOR HORSES: A watering trough will be filled by the park rangers if you call Alamo Lake State Park and give advance notice of your arrival date. Water is available at Campground C, 300 yards from the equestrian area, but you must bring buckets or containers as horses should not be taken into this area. Of course, there is water in the lake 1/4 mile from the equestrian campgrounds.

CORRALS: None. However, a 40-foot long metal hitching post is provided. As many as 8 horses could be tethered overnight here.

OTHER FACILITIES: Comfort stations, showers, hot water, and night lighting in Campground C on Cholla Road, just south of the equestrian campground, can be used.

ACCESS: Travel west of Phoenix on U.S. Highway 60 (Grand Avenue) to Wickenburg. Continue straight through town and under the overpass (do not turn north on Highway 93 to Kingman). Travel to mile post 61.6 in Wenden, turn north (right) on Alamo Dam Road, and travel approximately 35 more miles to Alamo Lake State Park. After passing the state park ranger booth on the right, watch for Cholla Road, also on the right. Turn right toward the lake, on Cholla Road, passing Campground C on the right. Turn left into Camp-ground D. Select a site near the hitching post (down a slope to the west).

(Continued)

Alamo Lake State Park Trails

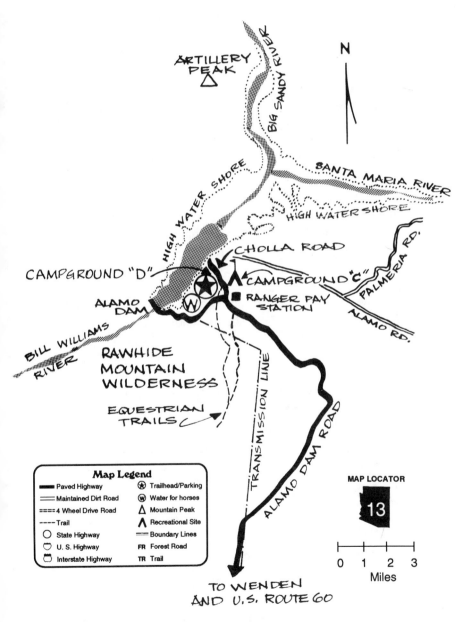

DESCRIPTION: There are many trails at lake level, weaving in and out of the sandy washes, tamarack and willow. Of course, you can create your own trails because it's hard to get lost with the lake in full view from almost any vantage point.

The loop trail described here is on the south side of Alamo Lake and climbs in elevation to allow views of the lake, the dam, and all of the surrounding area. This trail is not signed so be sure to use this description and your park maps to stay on the trail.

Ride in a southerly direction out of the campsite on the left side of Cholla Road. Angle toward the ranger station and cross the main road to the park. On the south side of the main road is a "deer crossing" highway sign. The trail begins in a sandy wash just before this sign. Follow the trail up through the cholla and other cacti to the ridge that is paralleled by the power lines.

As you climb, the views of Alamo Lake unfold, and across the lake pointed, maroon-colored Artillery Peak becomes a prominent landmark.

The trail continues south to reach a junction with the trail on the left that takes you back down to the main road. Pass this trail by and continue on to a higher plateau with many rock outcroppings. This is the half-way point, approximately 2 hours from the trailhead, and a good stopping place for a rest. Take time to enjoy the panoramic view of the entire lake and surrounding area. When you are ready to return, descend until you reach the junction of the trail you rode on the way up the hill. Take the trail to the right, which brings you back to the main road. When you reach the paved road, cross it and follow the trail on the north side into a big wash. In approximately .25 mile this wash takes you along the side of Campground D. When you find a place that you can safely ride up the side of the wash, return to the campground.

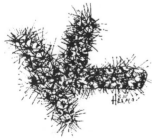

Nesting bald eagles are frequently seen in the canyon below Alamo Dam, and wild burros scamper on all of the hillsides here.

NOTE: Cholla cacti grow profusely along these trails. Bring combs to remove cacti segments from yourself or from your horse.

"Jumping" cholla cactus

MAP LOCATOR

14

Black Canyon Trail
Emery Henderson Trailhead

LOCATION: 5 miles north of Carefree Highway in Phoenix just west of I-17 at the New River exit on the road to Lake Pleasant.

LENGTH: 6-7 miles one way   **COUNTY:** Maricopa

USE: Light to Moderate   **SEASON:** Oct. through April

RATING: Easy to Moderate   **ELEVATION:** 2,500' to 2,900'

USGS TOPO MAP: New River

CONTACT AGENCY: Maricopa County Parks and Recreation Department

HORSE TRAILER PARKING: Well-designed pull-through parking on paved parking lot with room for 10-12 horse trailers.

WATER FOR HORSES: None at this time.

CORRALS: None

OTHER FACILITIES: Well-planned facilities, including picnic ramadas, comfort stations, BBQ grills, and hitching posts for horses.

ACCESS: Travel north out of Phoenix on Interstate 17, and take Exit 232 at New River, 3 miles north of Desert Hills Equestrian Center. Turn west (left) on Lake Pleasant Road. Travel 2.7 miles to the Emery Henderson Trailhead on the north side of the road. This newly dedicated trailhead was constructed with Heritage Fund monies and was named in honor of one of Arizona's leaders in trail development for equestrians.

DESCRIPTION: The Black Canyon Trail winds its way north from Phoenix to Mayer. It was originally a route used by ranchers and settlers for cattle and sheep drives. The trail crosses the Agua Fria River and passes near Rock Springs, Black Canyon City, Bumble Bee and Cordes as it heads north.

The trail is well-defined and marked for the first 6 miles. Return to trailhead at point indicated on map. A future loop trail is planned for this trailhead. This trail's close proximity to the city makes it an easy-to-reach and enjoyable destination for a 3-4 hour remote area ride.

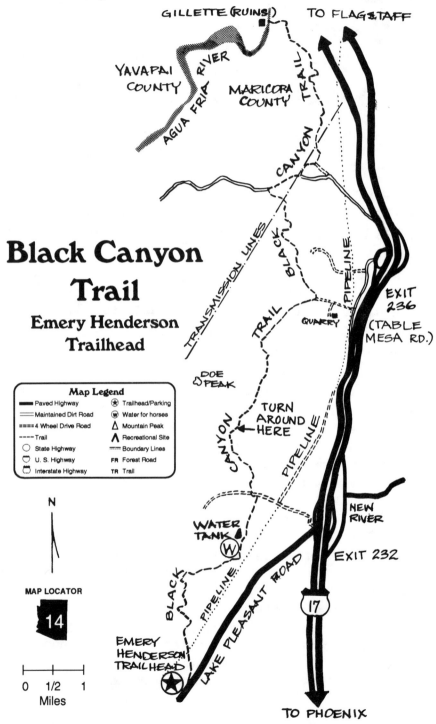

GILLETTE (RUINS)

TO FLAGSTAFF

YAVAPAI
COUNTY

AGUA FRIA RIVER

MARICOPA
COUNTY

CANYON TRAIL

Black Canyon
Trail
Emery Henderson
Trailhead

TRANSMISSION LINES

BLACK

PIPELINE

TRAIL

QUARRY

EXIT
236

(TABLE
MESA RD.)

DOE
PEAK

TURN
AROUND
HERE

CANYON

PIPELINE

Map Legend

▬▬ Paved Highway	✪ Trailhead/Parking
▭▭▭ Maintained Dirt Road	ⓦ Water for horses
▪▪▪▪ 4 Wheel Drive Road	△ Mountain Peak
---- Trail	⋀ Recreational Site
◯ State Highway	▭▭▭ Boundary Lines
▽ U. S. Highway	FR Forest Road
⬠ Interstate Highway	TR Trail

N

MAP LOCATOR

14

0   1/2   1
Miles

WATER
TANK
ⓦ

NEW
RIVER

BLACK

PIPELINE

LAKE PLEASANT ROAD

EXIT 232

17

EMERY
HENDERSON
TRAILHEAD
✪

TO PHOENIX

15

Cave Creek Recreation Area Trails

LOCATION: 20 miles north of Phoenix. Entrance is north of the intersection of Carefree Highway and 32nd Street.

LENGTH: Varies with trail(s)   **COUNTY:** Maricopa

USE: Light to Moderate   **SEASON:** Oct. though April

RATING: Moderate to Difficult   **ELEVATION:** 2,000' to 2,600'

USGS TOPO MAP: Cave Creek, New River SE

CONTACT AGENCY: Maricopa County Parks and Recreation, Cave Creek Recreation Area.

HORSE TRAILER PARKING: Very well-planned equestrian use area at the end of the park road, with ample turn-around parking in gravelled area. Day parking fees may be charged.

WATER FOR HORSES: Spigots available at trailhead. Bring your own buckets.

CORRALS: None.

OTHER FACILITIES: Comfort stations, picnic tables, BBQ grills, lighting, drinking water.

ACCESS: Travel north of Phoenix on Interstate17 to Carefree Exit 223 and go east on Carefree Highway approximately 6.3 miles to 32nd Street. Turn north on 32nd Street and follow the signs to the park entrance. After entering the park pass the group area, picnic ramadas and playgrounds on Tonalite Drive. The equestrian staging area is at the end of this road on the north side. Many of the trails start at this staging area.

DESCRIPTION: The Cave Creek Recreation Area was opened in 1992, but some of the trails have been in the park area for a number of years. Equestrians can choose from a network of trails that vary in distance and terrain. The trails intersect each other in several locations, providing different combinations of loop trails within the 3,000 acres that comprise the recreation area. This higher elevation north of the Valley of the Sun offers slightly cooler temperatures and

(Continued)

Cave Creek
Recreation Area Trails

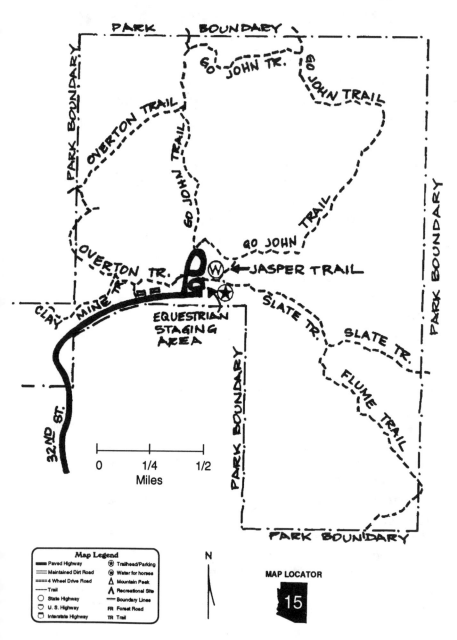

excellent views of Pinnacle Peak, New River and Black Mesa. There are hidden valleys peppered with old mining claims, tunnels, and shafts. The recreation area becomes a desert flower garden in March and April.

Two trails start at the northeast end of the staging area. They begin at a point parallel to the paved road that passes the restrooms. The Slate Trail starts at the east end of the equestrian staging area and exits at the park boundary in 1.6 miles.

A fork to the left (north) near the staging area is the Jasper Trail, only 0.2 miles, which connects to Go John Trail. Go John Trail is a 4.8 mile loop trail which can be ridden in either direction.

The Flume Trail (1.5 miles) forks to the right (south) off of the Slate Trail and ends at the park boundary.

The shortest loop ride (3 miles) begins at the Go John Trailhead located at the end of the most northern passenger vehicle parking area. Take this trail northward to the intersection with Overton Trail. Turn left, circle the north side of the mountain and return to the equestrian parking area at Tonalite Drive just north of the playground and ramadas.

The 4WD road at the southeastern end of the staging area goes up to the old Chrysocolla mine and dead ends.

Most of the trails in this area were developed in the past to reach old turquoise, tonalite, and talc mining claims, including the Mormon Girl and Phoenix Mines that produced a lot of ore in earlier years.

The recreation area has 6 upper ramadas and 4 lower ramadas. Ramadas and group areas may be reserved for special events or overnight use. However, the restrooms are locked between 6:00 p.m. and 6:00 a.m. while the recreation area is closed. **Horses must remain in the staging area and are not permitted in the ramada areas.** There is a campground host during the months of October-May when the recreation area is officially open. However, equestrians can access the trails year round through the equestrian gates provided along the park's perimeter fence line.

Raccoon

Dreamy Draw Trails

Charles M. Christiansen & Perl Charles Trails

LOCATION: Phoenix urban trails system, in Northern Avenue and 19th Street area.

LENGTH: 4.8 to 11 miles one way **COUNTY:** Maricopa

USE: Heavy **SEASON:** Oct. through April

RATING: Moderate to Difficult **ELEVATION:** 1,500' to 1,800'

USGS TOPO MAP: Sunnyslope, Paradise VAlley

CONTACT: City of Phoenix, Parks, Recreation and Library Department

HORSE TRAILER PARKING: Adequate staging area in dirt parking lot before the picnic ramadas for 10-12 horse trailers. Staging area has hitching posts and pull-through parking is available in parking lot unless it is crowded with many trailers. Alternate parking and turn-around at end of paved road in picnic ramada parking area.

WATER FOR HORSES: There is a water trough across the paved road at the entrance to the picnic area beside the horse staging area. There is also a spigot for water if you bring your own buckets.

CORRALS: None

OTHER FACILITIES: Comfort stations, ramadas, BBQ grills, drinking water, outdoor lighting.

ACCESS: Travel north (or south) on the Squaw Peak Parkway in Phoenix and take the exit to Northern Avenue. Turn east on Northern (from the north you will go under the Parkway). Dreamy Draw Park road will appear immediately on the right. Turn right to enter the Park. The horse staging parking lot will be the first parking area you will reach.

DESCRIPTION: Charles Milo Christiansen was Phoenix Parks and Recreation Department Director for nine years and was instrumental in the efforts to create the Phoenix Mountain Preserve within

(Continued)

Dreamy Draw Trails

Charles M. Christiansen
and
Perl Charles Trails

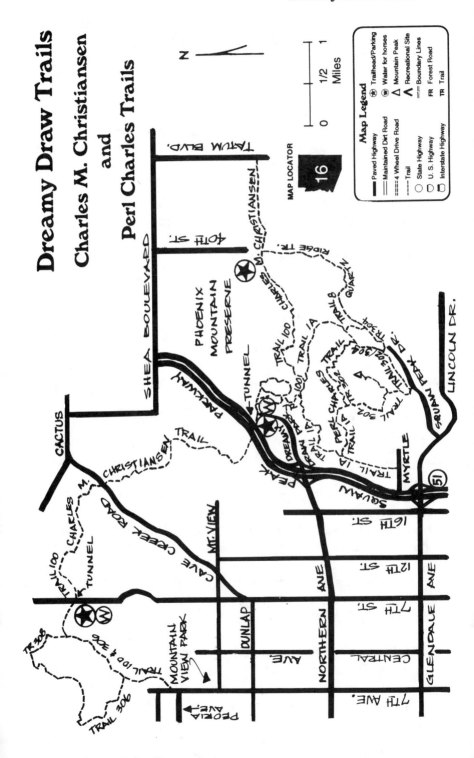

MAP LOCATOR

16

Map Legend

▬▬ Paved Highway	✶ Trailhead/Parking
▬ Maintained Dirt Road	Ⓦ Water for horses
═══ 4 Wheel Drive Road	△ Mountain Peak
- - - Trail	∧ Recreational Site
◯ State Highway	▬ Boundary Lines
Ⓤ U. S. Highway	FR Forest Road
▭ Interstate Highway	TR Trail

0   1/2   1
Miles

N

the central urban area of the city. The preserve has a vast network of interlacing trails that offers miles of unrestricted trail riding for equestrians. The trail given his name is 11 miles in length, beginning at Mountain View Park at the west end and terminating on the east side of the park at Tatum Boulevard.

This staging area is well-positioned to ride this trail in either direction. Follow Trail #100 through the preserve. Heading west takes you past the Maricopa County Sheriff's Office stables and arena, just north of the Pointe at Tapatio Cliffs resort, and ends at Mountain View Park at 7th Avenue and Peoria. Heading east, the trail takes you to a labyrinth of intersecting trails.

The City of Phoenix has numbered all of the main trails in the preserve and all intersections are marked. When city streets intersect the trails, there are large metal culverts with plenty of clearance for mounted equestrians that continue the trails safely under the streets.

Perl Charles Trail

DESCRIPTION: Perl Charles was an equestrian who loved the Phoenix urban mountains and was very instrumental in helping to preserve the trails and mountains in this area of the city. To reach this trail, follow Trail #100 (Charles M. Christiansen Trail) east 0.8 mile to the junction on the right with the Perl Charles Trail. Pass this first junction and continue another 0.2 mile to the second intersection. Turn right here and follow the Perl Charles Trail markers. There will be many trails criss-crossing the Perl Charles Trail, so be sure to watch carefully for the horseshoe insignia sign that marks the trail. The trail heads southeast and climbs along the north side of Squaw Peak and then briefly joins the Nature Trail #304 and the Circumference Trail #302 to go over a high pass. The trail then descends into Hidden Valley and leaves the Circumference Trail to cross Hidden Valley and rejoin the Christiansen Trail. This loop ride is 4.8 miles. Return to the Dreamy Draw Trailhead following the signs on the Christensen Trail #100, which is 0.8 mile back through the tunnel to the horse staging area.

MAP LOCATOR

Estrella Mountain Regional Park Trails

LOCATION: Approximately 18 miles west of Phoenix on Interstate 10 at the Estrella Parkway Exit 126 and 7 miles south of Interstate 10.

LENGTH: Varies with trail(s) **COUNTY:** Maricopa

USE: Light to Moderate **SEASON:** Oct. through April

RATING: Easy to Moderate **ELEVATION:** 900' to 1,900'

USGS TOPO MAP: Avondale SW/Buckeye

CONTACT AGENCY: Maricopa County Parks and Recreation Department, Estrella Mountain Regional Park

HORSE TRAILER PARKING: Ample pull-through parking available at the trailhead and around the rodeo arena area adjacent to the trailhead. Day parking fees may be charged.

WATER FOR HORSES: A water spigot is located outside the rodeo arena on the southeast end. No water trough is provided.

CORRALS: None. There are hitching posts outside the rodeo arena for public use.

OTHER FACILITIES: Comfort stations, ramadas, public water, lighting, rodeo arena and stock pens.

ACCESS: From Phoenix travel west toward Los Angeles on Interstate 10 for approximately 18 miles. Take Estrella Parkway Exit 126, turn south (left) and go approximately 7 miles. When you cross over the Gila River bridge, turn east (left) on Vineyard Road. Go through the park entrance, and continue on Vineyard Road past the golf course, ramadas, and picnic areas to the end of the road, which is at the trailhead and the large rodeo arena. The park can also be entered from the north on Bullard Avenue.

DESCRIPTION: There are two trailheads and four horse trails that start at the rodeo arena area. The trails are marked with letters A through E, and there are colored trail marker tags that match the colors of the trails shown on the map at the trailhead.

(Continued)

Estrella Mountain Regional Park Trails

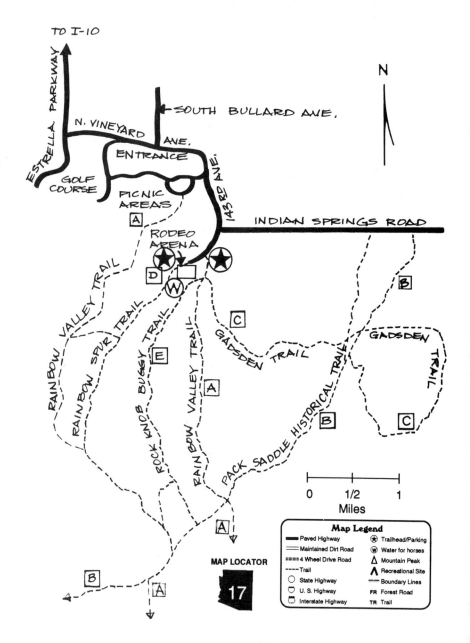

Trail E begins on the east side of the rodeo arena and is soon joined by trails A and C. Trail D begins at the west side of the arena, behind the grandstand and the announcer's booth.

Trail A, the *Rainbow Valley Trail,* is the longest (15.7 miles) and one of the more difficult trails, as it skirts around many of the higher peaks and has the most up-and-down hill riding in the park. This was a favorite route of horseback and stage coach travelers who were going from the Colorado River to Phoenix and Prescott in the 1800's.

Trail B, the *Pack Saddle Historical Trail,* is reached by riding out on Trail A until it intersects Trail B. Trails A, C, and E all intersect Trail B, but at different locations. The Pack Saddle Trail angles across the park from northeast to southwest and is 5.2 miles in length. This trail stays on flatter terrain and must be reached by riding one of the other trails. This trail is designated as a State Historic Trail because it was part of an early wagon road between Phoenix and Rainbow Valley.

Trail C, the *Gadsden Trail,* is a nice 7.2 miles in length for a 3-4 hour ride. It has an inner loop that cuts the trail length in half for a shorter ride. You reach this trail by riding out on trail E from the eastern trailhead.

Trail D, the *Rainbow Spur Trail,* is a short 1.7 miles that starts out west of the arena and makes a nice connecting point to ride many of the trails on the western side of the Park.

Trail E, the *Rock Knob Buggie Trail,* is 2.8 miles in length, and is a wider trail intended for horse-drawn buggies and wagons. It crosses a few sandy washes, but is otherwise quite flat and not as interesting as the other trails. This trail does have a picnic table, comfort station, and hitching post about half way out from the trailhead.

SPECIAL NOTE: Estrella Mountain Regional Park is open from 6:00 a.m. to 10:00 p.m. daily. To schedule an overnight group event, call Maricopa County Parks and Recreation Department and make reservations. The exceptionally large equestrian area makes this facility ideal for evening and weekend group events.

Gambel's Quail

Jacob's Crosscut Trail

LOCATION: East of Phoenix and 5 miles north of Apache Junction just east of Lost Dutchman State Park in the Tonto National Forest.

LENGTH: 6.3 miles one way   **COUNTY:** Maricopa and Pinal

USE: Moderate to Heavy   **SEASON:** Nov. through March

RATING: Easy   **ELEVATION:** 2,200'

USGS TOPO MAP: Goldfield

CONTACT AGENCY: Tonto National Forest, Mesa Ranger District; Lost Dutchman State Park

HORSE TRAILER PARKING: Ample turn-around parking just north of Lost Dutchman State Park on FR78, the First Water Trailhead road. Park in large dirt parking area on the south (right) side of the road, 0.6 mile from Route 88.

WATER FOR HORSES: None at trailhead. Intermittent water runs in the washes on the trail after it rains. Lost Dutchman State Park has spigots in the campground area. Bring buckets.

CORRALS: None

ACCESS: Travel east of Phoenix to Apache Junction on U.S. Highway 60 to Exit 196, Idaho Road and State Route 88, and go north toward Canyon Lake 5.3 miles. Pass the entrance to Lost Dutchman State Park and go 1/4 mile to FR78. Turn right off the paved highway onto this dirt road and travel 0.6 miles and park just north of the wash in the parking area on the right side of the road. The trail begins at the southwest corner of the parking area. Look for the Forest Service sign designating Trail #58.

DESCRIPTION: This trail winds its way through the gentle slopes at the western, picturesque end of the Superstition Mountains. It makes a nice leisurely day ride over easy terrain through washes and over small rises, with the Superstitions rising dramatically off the desert floor right beside the trail.

From the northern end of the trail, the route takes you between Lost Dutchman State Park and the Superstition Wilderness boundaries to the end of the trail at Broadway Road, for a total of 6.3 miles one way. The trail crosses a number of hiking trails out of Lost Dutchman State Park. These trails are designated for hikers only, so be sure to stay on Trail #58 at these intersections.

For a shorter ride, turn around anywhere on the trail to return to the trailhead, as this is not a loop route. The trail is a mixture of soft, easy, sandy ground with rocky sections on some of the slopes.

Jacob's Crosscut Trail

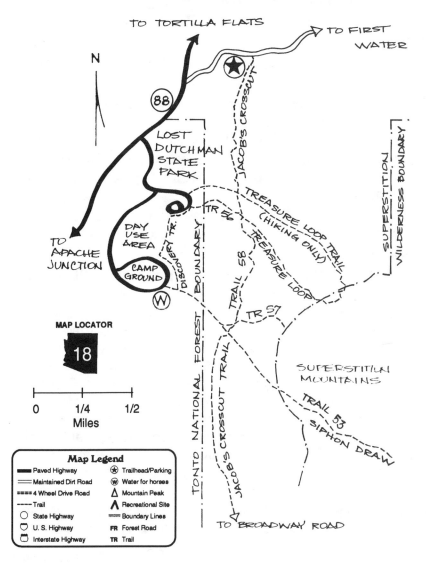

McDowell Mountain Regional Park Trails

LOCATION: 15 miles northeast of Scottsdale, 4 miles north of Fountain Hills on McDowell Mountain Road.

LENGTH: Varies with trail(s)   **COUNTY:** Maricopa

USE: Moderate   **SEASON:** Oct. through April

RATING: Easy to Moderate   **ELEVATION:** 1,600' to 2,900'

USGS TOPO MAP: McDowell Peak/Fort McDowell

CONTACT AGENCY: Maricopa County Parks and Recreation, McDowell Mountain Regional Park

HORSE TRAILER PARKING: Ample pull-through parking for 30-50 horse trailers in a large parking lot designed for equestrian use. Hitching posts are scattered around the parking area. Day parking fees may be charged.

WATER FOR HORSES: Bring your own bucket. Water spigots are provided in several locations in the parking lot.

CORRALS: None

OTHER FACILITIES: Comfort stations, picnic tables, BBQ grills, ramadas, overnight camping permitted.

ACCESS: Travel north toward Scottsdale on any major street to Shea Boulevard and turn east. Go approximately eleven miles east of the intersection of Scottsdale Road and Shea to the traffic light at Fountain Hills Boulevard, turn north and travel through Fountain Hills, going past the golf course and lake with the fountain. Continue on Fountain Hills Boulevard until it ends at McDowell Mountain Road. Turn right on McDowell Mountain Road and travel north 4 miles to the entrance road to McDowell Mountain Regional Park on the west (left). Follow this paved road about 2 miles to Shallmo Drive and turn right. The equestrian staging area is about 300 yards ahead.

DESCRIPTION: The proximity of this high desert trails area to urban equestrians makes this one of the most desirable destina-

(Continued)

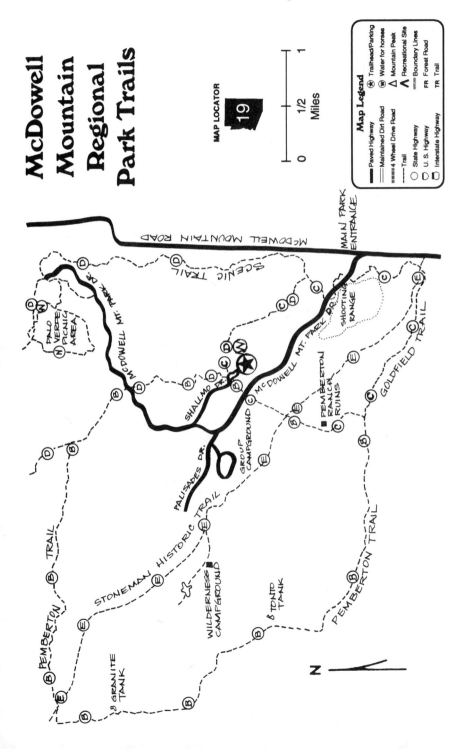

tions for day rides in the state. Many horseback riders seek these trails for their peace and solitude.

Three trails in the park are ideal for equestrians and all originate from the staging area. Maricopa County has marked the trails with letters at various locations and at trail intersections. Casual trails also will cross the main trails at various locations. Check your map frequently to prevent making incorrect turns. This is a large park, over 21,000 acres, so you may see some other equestrians, but the trails are not overcrowded.

The trails can be combined to make loops of varying lengths.

Trail B, the *Pemberton Trail* is 15.3 miles in length. This trail takes riders near the old remains of Pemberton Ranch which is just east of the trail 20 minutes from the trailhead.

Trail C, the *Goldfield Trail,* is 8.1 miles in length

Trail D, the *Scenic Trail,* 11.6 miles in length.

Trail E, the *Stoneman Historical Trail* is shown on many maps, but it is not marked or signed in the park.

Animal Tracks you may see on Arizona's trails

Antelope

Mule / Whitetail deer

Elk

Javelina

Mountain Sheep

H F   *Skunk*

H F   *Porcupine*

H   F *Bear*

H   F *Beaver*

H   F *Raccoon*

Domestic Dog or Coyote

Mountain Lion

Coatimundi

H = hind foot   F = forefoot

Seven Springs Recreation Area Trails

LOCATION: North of Phoenix, forty-five minutes north of Scottsdale on Cave Creek Road.

LENGTH: Varies with the trail(s) **COUNTY:** Maricopa

USE: Moderate to Heavy **SEASON:** Sept. through May

RATING: Moderate to Difficult **ELEVATION:** 2,600' to 3,360'

USGS TOPO MAP: Humboldt Mountain, New River Mesa

CONTACT AGENCY: Tonto National Forest, Cave Creek Ranger District

HORSE TRAILER PARKING: Two good pull-through and turn-around parking areas beyond the CCC Campgrounds and picnic areas, at the trailhead for Cave Creek Trail #4.

WATER FOR HORSES: Cave Creek runs year-round, and it is crossed several times on the trail. There are concrete stock tanks on some of the longer loop trails, as well.

OTHER FACILITIES: Comfort stations and picnic tables are available in the campgrounds. Horses are allowed only in undeveloped camping areas. New equestrian trailhead facilities are being planned.

ACCESS: From the east side of Phoenix travel north on either Pima Road or Scottsdale Road to their junction with Cave Creek Road. Turn right (east) on Cave Creek Road. From the west side of Phoenix travel north on I-17 to Carefree Road Exit 223. Travel east on Carefree Road to Scottsdale Road, turn north (left) to the junction with Cave Creek Road. Turn right (east) on Cave Creek Road.

The road forks in 6 miles. The right fork is FR 205 (Horseshoe Dam Rd.) to Bartlett Dam and Reservoir (Lake). Stay left on FR 24 to Seven Springs Recreation Area. The pavement ends 2.5 miles after this junction, except for a paved section that passes through a residential area. The trailhead is 6 miles after this short section of paved road. The road is narrower the last 2 miles before the trailhead, and there are several stream crossings over concrete

(Continued)

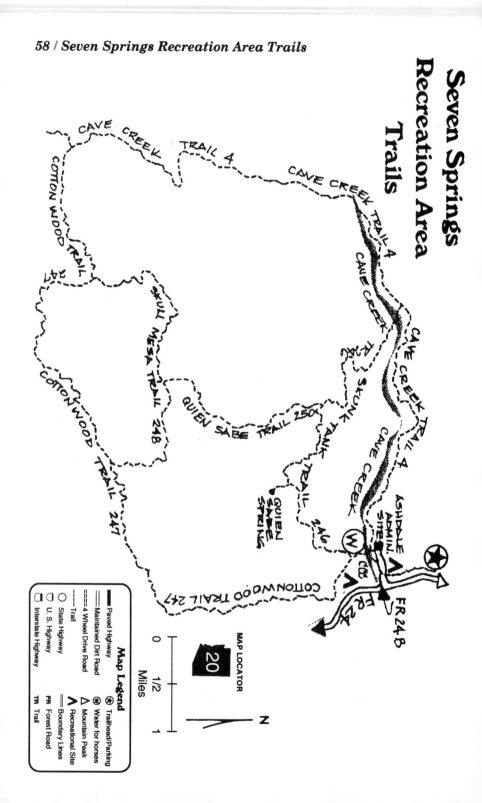

roadbeds in the campground area just before the trailhead parking lots. The trailhead is signed and on the west side of the road after passing the entrance to the CCC Campground. A second parking area is just beyond the trailhead parking area for overflow vehicles. Both parking areas may be used by equestrians.

DESCRIPTION: There are 30 miles of trails in the Cave Creek trail system that offer many one and two-day loop rides. The loop described here is approximately 8.8 miles in length.

From Cave Creek Trailhead, take Cave Creek Trail #4 (10.1 miles in length) south (there is a short spur to the CCC Campground.) After a mile the trail crosses FR 24 B and turns west. The trail takes a loop detour around a hiker's gate and drops down into a shady, tree-lined riparian area rich with scenic beauty and wildlife. The trail crosses Cave Creek Wash which usually has water in it.

Shortly after entering the riparian area the Ashdale Administration Center's fence line borders the trail and often there are horses and mules in the pastures. Be prepared to have some friendly equine onlookers gallop over to greet you!

There is one rocky area that can be challenging on the Cave Creek Trail approximately 3 miles from the trailhead. Sometimes this section has water in it and you have to ride through the water for 20 feet over large rocks. The Forest Service was working on this section so it is anticipated it will soon be improved.

After 4 miles Skunk Tank Trail #246 (4.8 miles in length) junctions on the left with Cave Creek Trail #4. Turn left and leave Trail #4. Skunk Tank Trail climbs above the Cave Creek streambed and after 4.8 miles drops back down, crosses Cave Creek, and rejoins the Cave Creek Trail to complete the loop to the trailhead.

You may select the Quien Sabe Trail (2.5 miles), Skull Mesa Trail (3.0 miles), or Cottonwood Trail (10.0 miles) to extend the length of your loop ride. The Skull Mesa Trail is the most difficult trail in the Seven Springs area.

21

South Mountain Regional Park Trails

LOCATION: In Phoenix metropolitan area, south of Baseline Road between 48th Street and 51st Avenue.

LENGTH: Varies with trail(s)   **COUNTY:** Maricopa

USE: Moderate to Heavy   **SEASON:** Oct. through April

RATING: Mod. to Very Difficult   **ELEVATION:** 1,400' to 2,400'

USGS TOPO MAP: Lone Butte, Guadalupe, Laveen

CONTACT AGENCY: City of Phoenix Parks, Recreation, and Library Department

HORSE TRAILER PARKING: Parking is available at the equestrian trailhead which is located at a left turn 0.2 mile after the park headquarters buildings. This parking area has pull-through parking and connects to the Ranger Trail and Crosscut Trail.

The best parking for the western end of the National Trail is 4.3 miles from the Central Avenue park entrance on San Juan Road. It is just after the 4.0 mile marker and on the north (right) side of the road. *Do not go to the end of San Juan Road, as there is no room to turn around with a horse trailer in the parking lot there.*

Pull-through or turn-around parking is also available at the eastern end of the National Trail at a paved parking lot on Pima Canyon Road, which is reached by driving south of Baseline Road on 48th Street. This parking lot is very crowded, and horse trailer parking is extremely limited.

Two other parking areas used frequently by local equestrians are located outside the park, but have trails that lead into the park. One is at the T-Bone Steakhouse on 19th Avenue south of Dobbins Road, and the other is at The Stables Bar and Restaurant beside the All Western Stables, on the north (right) side of Central Avenue after the final curve, just before the park entrance.

WATER FOR HORSES: The equestrian trailhead has a water trough and horse bathing platform.

(Continued)

South Mountain Regional Park Trails

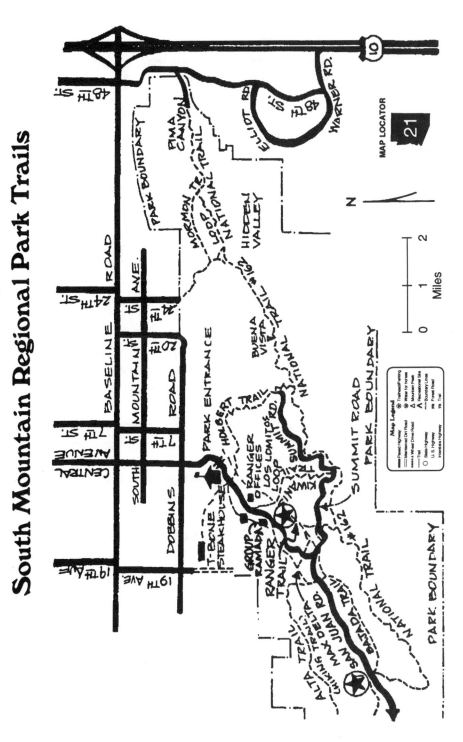

CORRALS: Day use round pen and hitching posts are located at the equestrian trailhead.

OTHER FACILITIES: There are many ramadas, BBQ grills, comfort stations, and picnic tables throughout the park. There is outdoor lighting around the group activity areas, in the parking lots and along the main entrance road. A small arena is planned for the equestrian trailhead.

ACCESS: From the south and eastern sides of Phoenix, travel to Baseline Road which is reached from Interstate 10, at Exit 155. Travel west on Baseline Road to Central Avenue. Turn south (left) on Central Avenue and follow the road until it curves and enters the park.

From the west and northern sides of Phoenix, travel on Interstate 10 and take the 7th Avenue Exit 144. Stay on the freeway access road at 7th Avenue, continue on to Central Avenue, (there is no freeway exit at Central Avenue) and turn south (right) on Central Ave. Continue on Central Avenue, past Baseline Road. Central Avenue curves and enters the Park.

The park may also be accessed at the eastern end by turning south off Baseline Road at 48th Street, which is very close to Interstate 10. This is a very busy parking area and it's often difficult to find parking for horse trailers, especially on weekends.

DESCRIPTION: This is the world's largest municipal park, a vast, extremely rugged desert mountain preserve with more than 40 miles of trails. There are eight main trails signed in the park, but there are a myriad of trails connecting the washes and lower slopes that can give hours of riding pleasure without ever climbing the more rugged mountain slopes.

The longest trail follows the ridges on top of South Mountain and runs east to west, skirting around the communications towers with the red lights that are a Phoenix landmark at night. This is the National Trail #162, which forms part of the Sun Circle Trail around the entire metropolitan Phoenix area. The National Trail is 14.25 miles in length and it literally runs end to end within park boundaries.

Starting the National Trail at the western end near San Juan Road and riding east is highly recommended, as there is less use of the trail and fewer mountain bikes at that end. The trail is too long for pleasure riders to ride in one day and return to the origination

(Continued)

point. This is a good trail to arrange for a shuttle pick up at the other end or plan to exchange vehicle keys midway with another team of riders.

There are four trails that start on the lower slopes and run up canyons to join the National Trail. *All are extremely difficult and some are dangerous for most equestrians,* but many people ride them, nevertheless. These trails run north to south, and all climb 600' to 900' to reach the National Trail. The Kiwanis Trail (1 mile), the Ranger Trail (1.4 miles) (which is the least difficult of these four trails), the Mormon Trail (1.1 miles) and the Holbert Trail (2 miles). The Kiwanis Trail is near the park entrance and probably the trail most frequently used to approach the National Trail at its mid-point.

The Bajada Trail is 3.2 miles and runs southwest at the base of South Mountain somewhat parallel to San Juan Road. Alta Trail is strictly for hiking.

There is an interesting lower elevation one hour loop ride that gives you a variety of scenic views and the typical characteristics of the trails at the quieter and less heavily traveled western portion of the park. Start this loop ride at the west side of the equestrian trailhead to the Ranger Trail. Follow the Ranger Trail to the intersection with the Bajada Trail (Trail Post #5) and turn west (right) on the Bajada Trail, which parallels and eventually crosses the paved Summit Road. **Carefully cross over Summit Road. Cars and bicycles travel at fast speeds on this road.** After crossing Summit Road the Max Delta Loop Trail (Trail Post #6) forks to the north (right). Follow the Max Delta Loop Trail, which crosses the paved San Juan Road (cross with care) and loops back toward the east park entrance. The Crosscut Trail will intersect the Max Delta Loop Trail (Trail Post #16). Turn right on the Crosscut Trail, crossing the main park entrance road with care. Follow the Cross-cut Trail back to the equestrian trail-head.

The trails in South Mountain Park are a combination of soft and sandy, to rocky on the slopes and in some of the washes. They are well established and maintained.

Urban serenity & views of the Estrellas

Usery Mountain Recreation Area Trails

LOCATION: 12 miles northeast of Mesa on Ellsworth Road which leads north into Usery Pass Road.

LENGTH: 3.8 to 6.9 mile loops   **COUNTY:** Maricopa and Pinal

USE: Moderate to Heavy   **SEASON:** Oct. through April

RATING: Mod. to Very Difficult   **ELEVATION:** 1,800' to 2,960'

USGS TOPO MAP: Apache Junction

CONTACT AGENCY: Maricopa County Parks and Recreation Department, Usery Mountain Recreation Area and Tonto National Forest, Mesa Ranger District

HORSE TRAILER PARKING: Ample pull-through and turn-around parking at the horse staging area at the end of the park road. Day parking fees may be charged.

WATER FOR HORSES: There are water spigots in the horse staging area. Bring your own buckets.

CORRALS: None

OTHER FACILITIES: Comfort stations, picnic tables and ramadas in the horse staging area.

ACCESS: Travel east from Phoenix toward Apache Junction on U.S. Highway 60. Turn north (left) at Exit 191, Ellsworth Road. Travel approximately 6 miles north (Ellsworth Road becomes Usery Pass Road) to the entrance of Usery Park which is on the east (right) side of the road. Go through the park to the end of the road where the horse staging area is located.

DESCRIPTION: There are three equestrian trails in this park — Blevins Trail (3.8 miles), the Pass Mountain Trail #282 (6.9 miles) and the Superstition Loop Trail (0.85 mile). All are loop trails that are accessed at the horse staging area.

All other trails in Usery Mountain Regional Park are for hikers only. The park closes at sunset.

(Continued)

Usery Mountain Recreation Area Trails

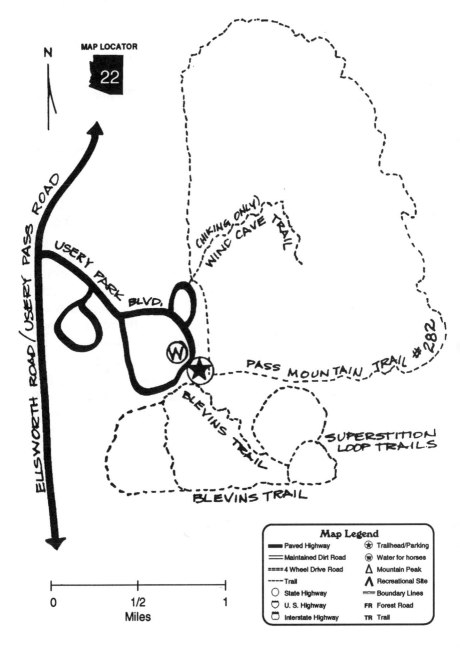

MAP LOCATOR

22

N

ELLSWORTH ROAD / USERY PASS ROAD

USERY PASS ROAD

USERY PARK BLVD.

(HIKING ONLY) WIND CAVE TRAIL

PASS MOUNTAIN TRAIL #282

BLEVINS TRAIL

SUPERSTITION LOOP TRAILS

BLEVINS TRAIL

W

Map Legend

▬▬ Paved Highway	⊛ Trailhead/Parking
═══ Maintained Dirt Road	Ⓦ Water for horses
==== 4 Wheel Drive Road	△ Mountain Peak
----- Trail	Λ Recreational Site
◯ State Highway	▭▭ Boundary Lines
⬭ U. S. Highway	FR Forest Road
▭ Interstate Highway	TR Trail

0   1/2   1
Miles

There is a target practice range near the entrance to the park, so the sound of shooting can be faintly heard on several of the trails, detracting somewhat from the peace and serenity of the area.

Blevins Trail begins on the west end of the staging area and passes through some lush high Sonoran Desert terrain with excellent views of the Goldfield and Superstition Mountains. The trail remains fairly flat and stays within park boundary lines. This moderately easy trail crosses many sandy washes and has several sections that are dirt roads.

The Superstition Loop Trail intersects the Blevins Trail and circles around several peaks. This trail climbs steeply over a ridge.

Pass Mountain Trail is extremely difficult and in some areas dangerous. Only the most experienced trail horses and equestrians should attempt to ride this trail, because it follows some rock ledges that can be slick under horseshoes. It is hoped some of the more dangerous areas will soon be significantly improved. The park recommends riding the trail counterclockwise, taking the trail to the south (right) where it splits shortly after leaving the parking area. Most of the trail is in the Tonto National Forest and Maricopa County. The Pass Mountain Trail climbs 900 feet to provide some spectacular views of distant mountain ranges including the Mazatzals, Four Peaks, McDowells and Superstitions. There are some steep grades and rocky areas that are extremely challenging on this trail. At the midway point the trail goes through a pass (elevation 2,590'). From here the terrain changes and the trail begins a gradual descent. ***You may want to dismount and walk your horse over the few slick rock areas on the trail. Remember, rain and its resulting erosion can quickly change trail conditions.***

Cactus Wren

MAP LOCATOR

White Tank Mountain Regional Park Trails

LOCATION: 15 miles west of Phoenix on Olive Avenue just west of Cotton Lane.

LENGTH: Varies with trail(s)   **COUNTY:** Maricopa

USE: Light to Moderate   **SEASON:** Oct. through April

RATING: Moderate to Difficult   **ELEVATION:** 1,580' to 2,400'

USGS TOPO MAP: White Tank Mountains SE/NE

CONTACT AGENCY: Maricopa County Parks and Recreation Dept.

FEES & HOURS: The park closes at sundown. Special arrangements must be made for evening or overnight use. Day parking fees may be charged.

HORSE TRAILER PARKING: Ample pull-through parking at the equestrian trailhead located approximately 2 miles from the park entrance on the right (east) side of the park road.

WATER FOR HORSES: The park provides a water trough at the equestrian trailhead.

CORRALS: None.

OTHER FACILITIES: Comfort stations, picnic tables, ramadas, BBQ grills, and drinking water. Horses are not permitted in picnic areas.

ACCESS: If you are traveling from the south or east side of Phoenix, take Interstate 10 west toward Los Angeles. Take Exit 124, Cotton Lane north (right) and travel 7 miles to Olive Avenue. Turn west (left) on Olive Avenue and this will run right into White Tank Mountain Regional Park 3 miles ahead.

If traveling from the north, take Dunlap Ave. Exit 207 off Interstate 17, and turn west (right). Dunlap becomes Olive at 43rd Avenue. Continue on Olive Avenue and pass through the Cotton Lane intersection. The park entrance is 3 miles ahead.

(Continued)

White Tank Mountain Regional Park Trails

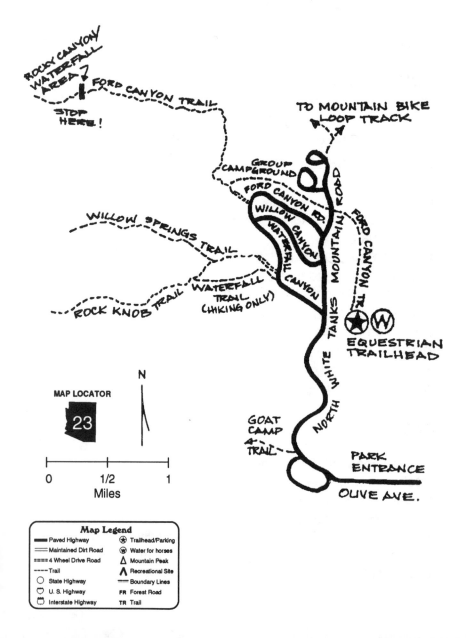

ROCKY CANYON WATERFALL AREA

STOP HERE!

FORD CANYON TRAIL

TO MOUNTAIN BIKE LOOP TRACK

GROUP CAMPGROUND

FORD CANYON RD.

WILLOW CANYON

WATERFALL CANYON

FORD CANYON TR.

WILLOW SPRINGS TRAIL

ROCK KNOB TRAIL

WATERFALL TRAIL (HIKING ONLY)

NORTH WHITE TANKS MOUNTAIN ROAD

EQUESTRIAN TRAILHEAD

GOAT CAMP TRAIL

PARK ENTRANCE

OLIVE AVE.

MAP LOCATOR

23

N

0   1/2   1
Miles

Map Legend

▬ Paved Highway	✪ Trailhead/Parking
═ Maintained Dirt Road	Ⓦ Water for horses
══ 4 Wheel Drive Road	△ Mountain Peak
--- Trail	Λ Recreational Site
◯ State Highway	▬ Boundary Lines
◯ U. S. Highway	**FR** Forest Road
◻ Interstate Highway	**TR** Trail

DESCRIPTION: The park has a system of trails that wind their way up the canyons into the White Tank Mountains. There are five horse trails and one trail for hikers only in the park. Mountain bikes are permitted on all horse trails. If you make advance reservations and pay a fee, a large group can gather for a ride from a gravel staging area just before the end of the park road on the west side. The trails are decomposed granite or sand in the lower canyons, with some rocky areas as the trail climbs.

Ford Canyon Trail is a good equestrian trail with interesting desert scenery. It is 4.4 miles long if you start at the north side of the equestrian trailhead. Use extreme caution when crossing the paved park road, which has frequent vehicular and bicycle traffic.

When you reach a steep downhill slope into a ravine with large rocks ahead on the left, stop and turn around. The trail becomes impassible for horses beyond this point and you will not be able to turn around. (See map.)

There are often pools of water collected in rock depressions from the rain and natural springs in the early spring season. The park's name possibly came from these small pools that reflect the sky and from above look like hundreds of small, sparkling water "tanks".

Spring wild flowers in the park are spectacular. There are trails in many of the canyons to explore, such as Willow Springs (2.8 miles), Goat Camp (3.0 miles), and Rock Knob (2.5 miles), so plan several visits.

Desert Cottontail

Lake Havasu City
Area Trails

LOCATION: Between Parker and Kingman on the eastern shores of the Colorado River, on U.S. Highway 95.

LENGTH: Varies with trail(s)   **COUNTY:** Mohave

USE: Moderate   **SEASON:** Oct. through April

RATING: Easy to Moderate   **ELEVATION:** 800' to 1,900'

USGS TOPO MAP: Lake Havasu City North and South

CONTACT AGENCY: Bureau of Land Management, Lake Havasu City

HORSE TRAILER PARKING: Limited turn-around at various access points to trails, depending upon other vehicles utilizing the parking space.

WATER FOR HORSES: None at trailhead areas. Casual water from springs seasonally available. Bring your own water.

CORRALS: None available.

OTHER FACILITIES: None.

ACCESS: Travel to Lake Havasu City from Phoenix by going west on Interstate 10 to Vicksburg Road Exit 45. Go north through the intersection with Highway 60, and turn left on State Highway 72 to Parker. At Parker turn north on U.S. Highway 95, which passes through Lake Havasu City and follows the Colorado River north toward Kingman. After passing the London Bridge and McCulloch Blvd., travel one mile north to Kiowa Blvd. Turn east (right) on Kiowa Blvd. and travel to Desert Garden Dr. Turn left, travel to Sycamore Way and turn right. Sycamore Way dead ends at the Havasu Equestrian Center, Inc. facilities.

From Flagstaff, travel west on Interstate 40 to Kingman. Turn south (left) on U.S. Highway 95 and travel to Lake Havasu City. Watch for Kiowa Blvd. on the east (left) side of the highway, and follow the access directions listed above.

DESCRIPTION: There are very active equestrians in Lake Havasu City and they have formed a non-profit association and built large boarding facilities for 160 members' horses, complete with a club-house, multiple arenas, round pens, foaling pens, etc. This group has developed an impressive system of trails leading into the mountains and washes in the northeastern outskirts of Lake Havasu City. The trails are on public land (Bureau of Land Management), but the equestrian association has no maps showing trail locations. If you want to ride the trails in this area, call ahead and get information and assistance from Lake Havasu Equestrians, 602-680-4448. The map shown below is provided to give you directions to the Equestrian Center, to identify two trailhead locations and to give some rather general indication of the trails.

NOTE: There is no overnight boarding available at the equestrian center. These facilities are for members only.

Lake Havasu Trails

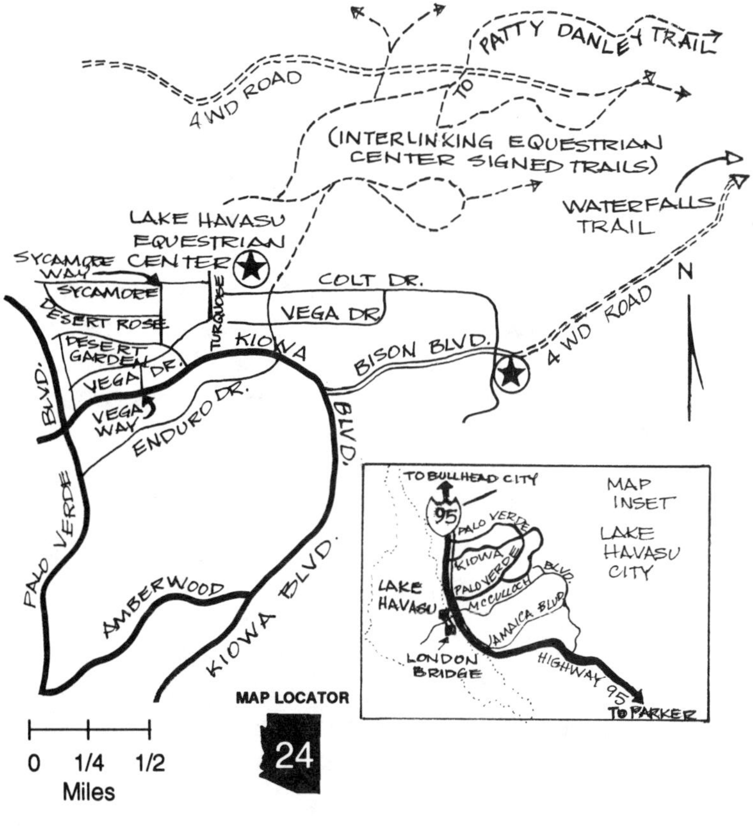

Pinetop – Lakeside Trails

Blue Ridge Trail

LOCATION: Most trails in the White Mountain Trail System are located near the towns of Pinetop and Lakeside off State Route 260, between Show Low and Springerville adjacent to Apache Sitgreaves National Forest.

LENGTH: 8.7 mile loop   **COUNTY:** Navajo

USE: Moderate   **SEASON:** May through Sept.

RATING: Moderate   **ELEVATION:** 6,600' to 7,400'

USGS TOPO MAP: Lakeside quadrants

CONTACT AGENCY: Apache Sitgreaves National Forest, Lakeside Ranger District

HORSE TRAILER PARKING: Pull-through parking at the Blue Ridge Trailhead No. 2. Another 2.8 miles down FR187 is a larger turn-around parking area at Trailhead No. 1. *Warning! This road can become muddy and impassable if wet!*

WATER FOR HORSES: There are intermittent, seasonal streams in the trail areas. Horses are not permitted in developed recreational areas around lakes. On the Blue Ridge Trail the southern section of the loop brings you right beside Billy Creek, where you can water your horse if seasonal water is available.

OTHER FACILITIES: None at trailheads. There are facilities at the equestrian centers on Porter Mountain Road and in Pinetop Lakes.

ACCESS: Travel east on State Route 260 to mile marker 355 and turn north (left) into Pinetop Lakes on Buck Springs Road. Travel approximately 0.6 mile to Tomahawk Road (Forest Road 182) with signage to Sky Hi Retreat Road. Turn northwest (left) on Tomahawk Road. Follow FR182 to the intersection of Forest Road 187 (1.8 miles), turn left and follow this road 0.2 mile to the trailhead. The Blue Ridge Trail may also be accessed from the trails leading into

(Continued)

Pinetop — Lakeside Trails
Blue Ridge Trail

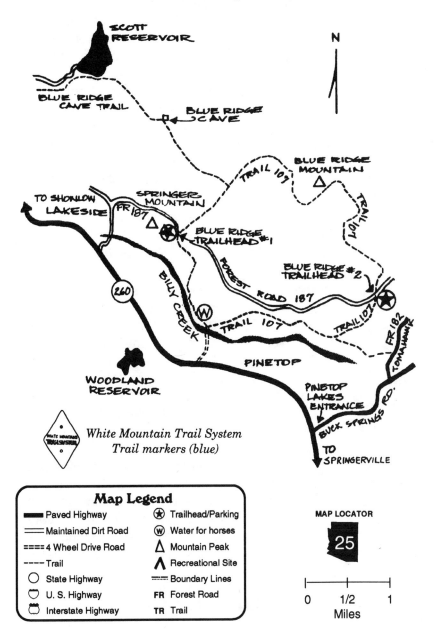

SCOTT RESERVOIR

N

BLUE RIDGE CAVE TRAIL

BLUE RIDGE CAVE

BLUE RIDGE MOUNTAIN

TRAIL 107

TO SHONLOW LAKESIDE

SPRINGER MOUNTAIN

FR 187

BLUE RIDGE TRAILHEAD #1

TRAIL 107

BLUE RIDGE TRAILHEAD #2

260

BILLY CREEK

FOREST ROAD 187

TRAIL 107

FR 182

TOMAHAWK

W

TRAIL 107

WOODLAND RESERVOIR

PINETOP

PINETOP LAKES ENTRANCE

BUCK SPRINGS RD.

*White Mountain Trail System
Trail markers (blue)*

TO SPRINGERVILLE

Map Legend

▬ Paved Highway	✪ Trailhead/Parking
═ Maintained Dirt Road	Ⓦ Water for horses
==== 4 Wheel Drive Road	△ Mountain Peak
---- Trail	∧ Recreational Site
○ State Highway	═══ Boundary Lines
▽ U. S. Highway	FR Forest Road
▭ Interstate Highway	TR Trail

MAP LOCATOR

25

0   1/2   1
Miles

and out of Scott Reservoir, as well as from the Porter Mountain Stables and the Pinetop Equestrian Center. (See Overnight Accommodations.)

DESCRIPTION: The Blue Ridge Trail (#107), is a loop trail with two trailheads. Access to the second trailhead is described above. The first trailhead is at the northwest end of the trail near Springer Mountain. The trail can be ridden in either direction from either trailhead. It has been marked with blue diamonds on the trees by the White Mountain Trail and Horsemen's Association. This trail is approximately 9 miles long if you ride the entire loop from either trailhead. If you ride from Porter Mountain Stables to the Scott Reservoir Trail, it will add another 3.5 miles to reach the loop trail. The trail connecting Scott Reservoir to the Blue Ridge Trail passes by the Blue Ridge Cave, a large underground cave that has been closed off. FR 187 bisects the loop trail. Both trailheads are located on this road.

The loop trail is very scenic and provides equestrians with a panorama of views and idyllic forest habitat. This destination for cool summer rides is a favorite retreat for desert-dwelling horseback enthusiasts.

Other trails in the White Mountain Trail System that provide additional equestrian opportunities include Country Club Trail #632 (3.5 miles long); Panorama Trail #635 (8 miles long); Timber Mesa Trail #636 (6 miles long); Buena Vista Trail #637 (9 miles long); Springs Loop Trail (3.8 miles long), Los Burros Trail #631 (13 mile loop); Juniper Ridge Trail #640 (7 or 14 mile loop); Los Caballos Trail #638 (14 mile loop); Land of Pioneers Trail #629 (11 mile loop); and the Ghost of the Coyote Trail #641 (16 mile loop). The White Mountain Trail System has received national recognition for its extensive series of loop trails, which are being interconnected to provide extended riding distances in this very scenic area. Contact the Lakeside Ranger District for maps and directions to the trailheads for these trails.

Rocky Mountain Wild Iris

26

Catalina State Park Trails

LOCATION: 6 miles north of Ina Road in Tucson on State Highway 77, to Globe.

LENGTH: Varies with trail(s)   **COUNTY:** Pima

USE: Moderate   **SEASON:** Oct. through April

RATING: Easy to Moderate   **ELEVATION:** 2,700' to 3,400'

USGS TOPO MAP: Oro Valley, Mt. Lemmon

CONTACT AGENCY: Arizona State Parks, Catalina State Park and Coronado National Forest, Santa Catalina Ranger District.

HORSE TRAILER PARKING: Ample pull-through parking at the Equestrian Center for 10-12 horse trailers.

WATER FOR HORSES: There is a water trough and spigot at the Equestrian Center.

CORRALS: There is a barn with 4 pipe corrals and 4 more open pipe corrals at the equestrian center. This is one of the most outstanding facilities for equestrians in the state.

OTHER FACILITIES: Comfort stations, picnic tables, BBQ grills, and water. There is a fee for day use and overnight camping.

ACCESS: Travel 6 miles north of Ina Road in Tucson on Oracle Road (State Highway 77). Near mile marker 81 turn east (right) into Catalina State Park. Go to the park ranger station and check in if you plan to overnight at the equestrian center. If you are only there for day use, stop at the ranger station to pay day-use fees. Turn left at the first road. Follow the signs to the equestrian center just beyond a trailer parking/camping area. If you plan to spend the night, you may want to unhitch the horse trailer and park it in the space beside the barn.

DESCRIPTION: The equestrian center has two trailheads. The Catalina Equestrian Trail, 1.4 miles in length that leaves the parking area at the south end, and the much longer 50-Year Trail, which

(Continued)

Catalina State Park Trails

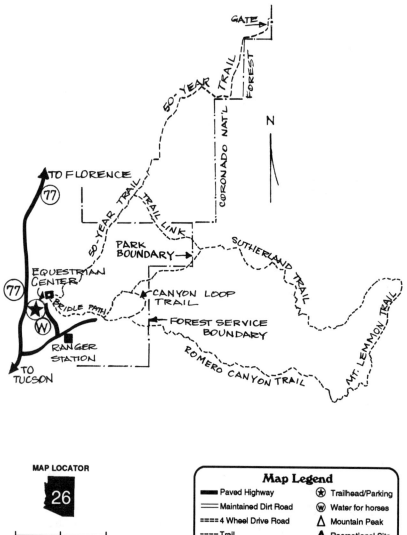

MAP LOCATOR

26

0	1/4	1/2

Miles

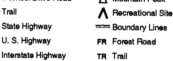

Map Legend

▬ Paved Highway		✪	Trailhead/Parking
═ Maintained Dirt Road		Ⓦ	Water for horses
==== 4 Wheel Drive Road		△	Mountain Peak
---- Trail		⋀	Recreational Site
○ State Highway		▭	Boundary Lines
♡ U. S. Highway		FR	Forest Road
⬠ Interstate Highway		TR	Trail

begins at the northeast end of the parking area.

The Catalina Equestrian Trail connects to the Canyon Loop, Romero Canyon and Sutherland Trails in the central area of the park. It is called the "Bridle Path" and is a flat, easy trail that winds its way at the back of the campsite and day-use areas in the park. The Canyon Loop Trail is 2.3 miles in length and makes a nice, short ride in the lower terrain of the park. *It is not recommended to continue on either the Romero Canyon or Sutherland Trails as they have some very narrow areas that are dangerous for equestrians.*

The 50-Year Trail is relatively new and approximately 8 miles one way. It is composed of a series of trails and 4-wheel-drive roads that are on a 50-year trail right-of-way use permit in an agreement negotiated between Pima County, the State Land Department and the land owner. This trail winds its way through rock formations that beckon for a role in a movie set. When you get to the fence line and gate which are at the entrance to the Coronado National Forest, it would be better to retrace your route to the trailhead. The trail through the Coronado National Forest has some trail markers, but it meets other trails at various points and has unmarked turns that are very confusing.

Cliff Chipmunk

Saguaro National Park

East Trails

LOCATION: On the east side of Tucson between Speedway and Broadway Blvds..

LENGTH: Varies with trail(s) **COUNTY:** Pima

USE: Moderate **SEASON:** Sept. through April

RATING: Easy to Very Difficult **ELEVATION:** 2,800' to 6,650'

CONTACT AGENCY: U.S. Department of the Interior, National Park Service, Saguaro National Park

USGS TOPO MAP: Tanque Verde Peak, Mica Mountain, Rincon Peak

HORSE TRAILER PARKING: Turn-around parking with wide road-side shoulders at two trailheads.

WATER FOR HORSES: None at trailheads. The Park has a large watering trough for horses at the junction of Three Tank Trail and Cabrillo Trail in the lower elevations. Water is also available in the higher elevations at Mica Tank and Aquila Tank (Three Tank Trail), Douglas Spring (Douglas Spring Trail) and Manning Camp (Manning Camp Trail).

CORRALS: There is one large corral that has been divided into three corrals at Manning Camp, a 19-mile one way overnight trip. You must pack in your own horse feed and check with the park ranger to make certain the Park Service horses are not using the corral facilities.

ACCESS: There are two entrances for equestrians to the national park, one off Broadway Blvd. and the other off Speedway Boulevard. (Two major east/west streets in Tucson.)

To reach the Cactus Forest Trailhead, travel east to the end of Broadway Blvd. The trailhead is located between the highway signs indicating "dead end" and "divided road." Use the dirt median to turn around and park in either direction on the wide shoulders.

(Continued)

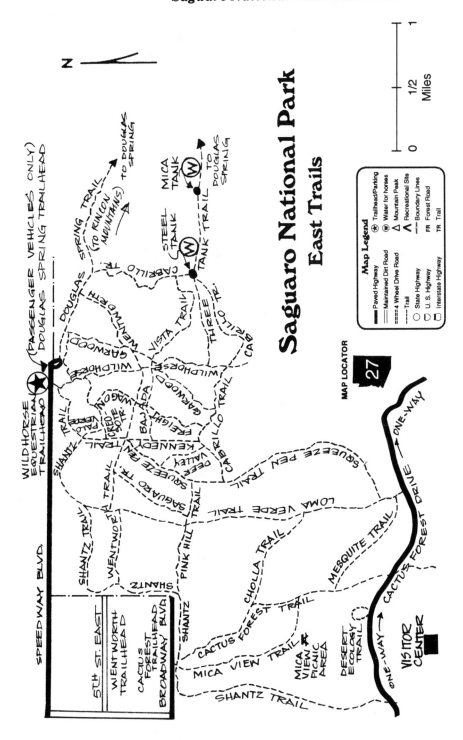

Saguaro National Park
East Trails

Map Legend

▬ Paved Highway	⊛ Trailhead/Parking
⸗ Maintained Dirt Road	Ⓦ Water for horses
┅┅ 4 Wheel Drive Road	△ Mountain Peak
┄┄ Trail	⸗ Boundary Lines
◯ State Highway	FR Forest Road
Ⓓ U.S. Highway	TR Trail
▣ Interstate Highway	△ Recreational Site

MAP LOCATOR

27

0   1/2   1
Miles

The Wildhorse Trailhead is on the south side of the road at the eastern end of Speedway Road. Park near the trailhead on the wide shoulder of the road, or go 100 yards more to the end, turn around and come back on the opposite side to park. (Paved parking lot at the end of Speedway is for passenger vehicles only.)

Both trailheads can accommodate 8-10 horse trailer rigs. Larger groups may contact the Park Service for special arrangements.

DESCRIPTION: Saguaro National Park is divided into two districts — Saguaro East, on the east side of Tucson, and Saguaro West, about 25 miles away on the west side of Tucson. Together, the two districts preserve 83,576 acres of the life and landscape of the Sonoran Desert. Both locations welcome equestrians to use the labyrinth of trails that traverse them.

The trails in the larger Saguaro East offer a wide variety of trail lengths and terrain. All the trails are well marked and signed. The lower trails are easy, the higher trails at the eastern end of the park are more rocky and difficult. Many trails interlink, offering a multitude of combinations.

A good 4-hour loop would be a combination linking the Shantz Trail, Pink Hill Trail, Cabrillo Trail, Douglas Spring Trail, Creosote Trail, and Wentworth Trail. Start and end this loop at the Cactus Forest Trailhead. The longer trails, Douglas Spring and Three Tank, go up into the Rincon Mountain foothills to the Douglas Spring Campground.

Horseback riding is permitted on all trails except the Tanque Verde Ridge Trail, Miller Creek Trail, and the Rincon Peak Trail. *The national park is very rugged in the Rincon Mountains. Check with a park ranger on trail conditions before riding into this backcountry.*

Overnight camping is allowed only at designated sites. Backcountry-use permits must be obtained in advance at the Visitor Center.

Majestic saguaros, abundant desert vegetation and a wide variety of wildlife make riding in the national park special and memorable.

A cool sip on Three Tanks Trail

Saguaro National Park

West Trails

LOCATION: West of Interstate 10 in Tucson, between Ina Road/ Picture Rocks Road on the north side and Kinney/Mile Wide Roads on the south side, near Old Tucson and the Arizona-Sonora Desert Museum.

LENGTH: 3.6 to 10.7 miles

COUNTY: Pima

USE: Moderate

SEASON: Oct. through April

RATING: Easy to Difficult

ELEVATION: 2,500' to 4,500'

CONTACT AGENCY: U.S. Department of the Interior, National Park Service, Saguaro National Park West

USGS TOPO MAP: Avra

HORSE TRAILER PARKING: Pull-through and turn-around parking for 4-5 horse trailers is available in Ez-kim-in-zan picnic area on Golden Gate Road. A 16-foot hitching post is located between the picnic area and Golden Gate Road.

WATER FOR HORSES: None that is dependable. There is intermittent water in the stream bed at King Canyon Spring which is near the intersection of King Canyon and Sendero Esperanza Trails.

CORRALS: None

OTHER FACILITIES: There are five designated picnic areas in the park. Each area has tables, grills, shade ramadas and comfort stations. They do not have drinking water. Red Hills Information Center, near the southern end of the park on Kinney Road, has additional information with updates on the trails.

ACCESS: Saguaro West can be reached from either the north or south side of Tucson. The north entrance to the park is reached by taking the Ina Road Exit 248 off Interstate 10 and traveling approximately 3.5 miles west to Wade Road. Turn south (left) on Wade Road which becomes Picture Rocks Road. At 1.6 miles from the turn on Wade Road there is a large dirt pullout for horse trailers on

(Continued)

Saguaro National Park

West Trails

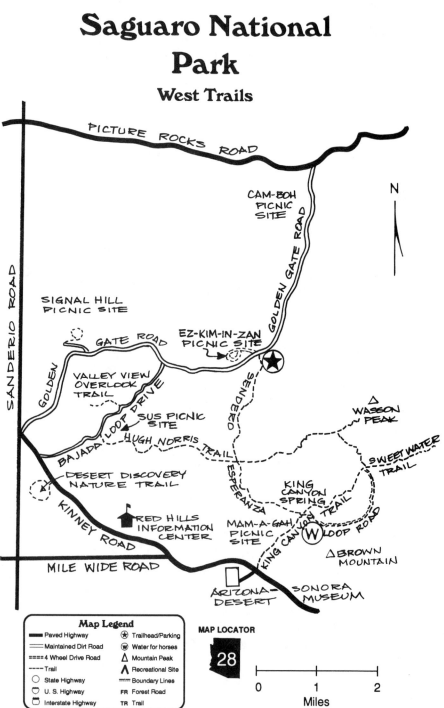

Map Legend

- ▬▬▬ Paved Highway
- ═══ Maintained Dirt Road
- ==== 4 Wheel Drive Road
- ----- Trail
- ○ State Highway
- ▽ U. S. Highway
- ⬭ Interstate Highway

- ✪ Trailhead/Parking
- Ⓦ Water for horses
- △ Mountain Peak
- ∧ Recreational Site
- ═══ Boundary Lines
- FR Forest Road
- TR Trail

MAP LOCATOR

28

0   1   2

Miles

the north side of the road. The pullout is in a large horseshoe bend in the road and is often used by equestrians to enter the national park. At 3.2 miles from the turn on Wade Road is a sign indicating a turn to the left on a dirt road that goes to Red Hills Visitor Center/ Scenic Drive. Turn left on this road (Golden Gate Road). It is a well-maintained road that loops through the park. Travel 2.7 miles on Golden Gate Road to the Ez-kim-in-zan Picnic Area. Enter the picnic area to park and unload your horse. The Sendero Esperanza Trail starts at a trailhead across Golden Gate Road from the picnic area. This trail connects to the other major trails in the park.

Equestrians can enter the park from the south by traveling on Interstate 10 to the exit for Interstate 19 to Nogales. Travel south 1.3 miles and take Exit 99 to Ajo Way. Turn west, following the signs to the Arizona-Sonora Desert Museum and Old Tucson. Follow Ajo Way 4.6 miles to the Kinney Road intersection. Turn north (right) on Kinney Road and travel approximately 9 miles, passing Old Tucson and the museum. Kinney Road goes to the Red Hills Information Center and on to Golden Gate Road. Bypass the Bajada Loop Drive, as there is no horse trailer parking along this road. Turn northeast (right) on Golden Gate Road. After you pass the other end of Bajada Loop Drive, you will come to the Ez-kim-in-zan Picnic Area which has equestrian use parking and hitching posts.

(Continued)

Saguaros silhouette their dominance over the trails in the park.

DESCRIPTION: The park is open 24 hours a day, and the trails are all open to equestrian use. This is primarily designated a wilderness area, so only horseback riders and hikers use these trails. *The upper portions of the Hugh Norris and King Canyon Trails to Wasson Peak are extremely steep and too narrow for equestrians,* but any of the other trails are excellent for hours of horseback enjoyment.

The Sendero Esperanza Trail is linked to many other trails within the national park and is an ideal trail from which to start. The Spanish name of this trail translates to "trail of hope" which no doubt referred to the mining activity in this area. The trail passes by the old Gould Copper Mine and many open mine shafts. *Be sure to stay on the established trails. These old shafts are dangerous and can cave in easily.*

The views from the trail include the tall peaks of Mt. Wrightson and Mt. Hopkins to the southeast and Kitt Peak to the south.

An enjoyable 4-5 hour loop ride that affords great views begins at the Ez-kim-in-zan Picnic Area trailhead to the Sendero Esperanzo Trail. This trail climbs to meet the Hugh Norris Trail, then descends to a junction with the King Canyon Trail. There is usually water for horses in King Canyon near the Mam-A-Gah Picnic Ramada. The loop continues up King Canyon Trail to the intersection of Sweetwater Trail and the trail to Wasson Peak. At this point a right turn will take you back down an old roadbed on the east side of King Canyon, which rejoins the Sendero Esperanza Trail near the Mam-A-Gah Picnic Ramada. Return to the trailhead via this trail.

The park is a protected haven for the mighty saguaros, monarchs of Arizona's desert. The best time to ride is in the cooler winter months and early spring when there is often a bountiful display of desert flowers. The saguaros bloom in late April and May. The blooms are beautiful, opening in the cool of night a few hours after sunset, and fading by the next afternoon.

Be sure to follow the national park regulations when riding these trails. No pets, even on leashes, are allowed on the trails. Be sure to secure personal belongings out of sight in locked vehicles and horse trailers when parking in the park.

MAP LOCATOR

Tucson Mountain Regional Park Trails

LOCATION: Approximately 6 miles west of Tucson off Interstate 10 and Interstate 19 to Nogales.

LENGTH: Varies with trail(s) **COUNTY:** Pima

USE: Moderate to Heavy **SEASON:** Winter

RATING: Easy to Moderate **ELEVATION:** 2,500' to 2,900'

USGS TOPO MAP: Cat Mountain, Brown Mountain

CONTACT AGENCY: Pima County Parks and Recreation Department

HORSE TRAILER PARKING: The best place to park is at the east side of the Park at the Starr Pass East Trailhead, which has a large clearing area for staging. On the west side of the Park the pull-off areas on Kinney Road provide other alternate areas for parking. Although Kinney Road has a lot of motor vehicle traffic, the pull-offs are quite wide and allow room for most horse trailers under 20 feet in length. There are over 25 such pull-offs and many are within several hundred yards of one of the trails in the Park.

WATER FOR HORSES: None provided within the park.

CORRALS: None

OTHER FACILITIES: None

ACCESS: Day use from 7:00 a.m. to 10:00 p.m. Travel to Tucson on Interstate 10 and take 22nd Street Exit 259. Drive west on 22nd Street (Starr Pass Blvd.) to the Starr Pass Resort/Development. Go 0.2 mile beyond the clubhouse (road curves north), and turn left (west) on the first dirt road. Follow this dirt road approximately 0.25 mile to the large clearing area for staging. Park boundary and the Starr Pass trail is 150 yards west at the end of a short section of jeep road. To reach the alternate western side of the park, travel on Interstate 10 to Exit 261 and go south toward Nogales on Interstate 19. Go 1.3 miles to Ajo Way Exit 99. Travel west on Ajo Way 5.2 miles to Kinney Road. Turn north (right) on Kinney Road 2.2 miles to the Park entrance.

(Continued)

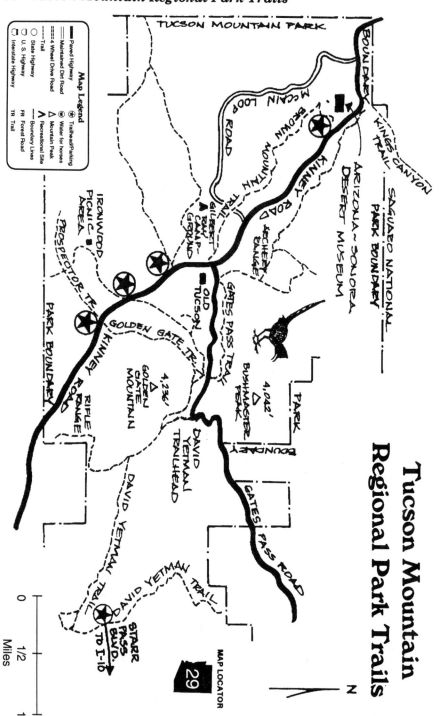

Tucson Mountain
Regional Park Trails

DESCRIPTION: The Tucson Mountains are not as high as the other mountains in the Tucson area, and offer excellent winter-season riding opportunities. There are many trails within the park boundaries, most of which are easily reached from Kinney Road, a paved road running diagonally from the southeast to the northwest in the park.

The longer trails are named, with many shorter, unnamed trails connecting with the main trails all through the park. The main trails are the Golden Gate Loop Trail (6.6 miles), Brown Mountain Trail Loop (5 miles), Prospector Trail (2 miles), David Yetman Trail (5.4 miles) and the Gilbert Ray Campground Trail Loop (5.3 miles).

The Golden Gate, Cat, and Brown Mountain peaks dominate the park. The trails meander around the base areas of the peaks through some very scenic desert landscape. There have been many movies filmed in the Old Tucson area near the Golden Gate Trail, including *Rio Bravo, Cimarron, Gunfight at the O.K. Corral,* and *Three Amigos.* Columbia Studios built Old Tucson Studios in 1939 to film the epic outdoor western, *Arizona.* In addition, the television series *Bonanza, Gunsmoke,* and *High Chaparral* were filmed in this area.

Use the map to select your route. One of the most popular loop trails is the 5.5 mile Golden Gate Trail that loops from Kinney Road toward Gates Pass Road, circles back toward Old Tucson, crosses Kinney Road, circles the Ironwood Picnic Area and returns via the Prospector Trail to Kinney Road. The Golden Gate Trail also connects with the David Yetman Trail (named after a member of the Pima County Board of Supervisors on his retirement).

Near the northwestern end of the park, close to the Arizona-Sonora Desert Museum, is the Brown Mountain Loop Trail, which has sections on both sides of Kinney Road. This trail is adjacent to the Juan Santa Cruz Picnic Area. The Gilbert Ray Loop (named after the first director of the Tucson Parks and Recreation Department) is close to the Old Tucson Studios and leads into the Gilbert Ray Campground area. This 5.3 mile loop heads west toward the park boundary and then circles back toward the campground. Equestrians, mountain bikes and an occasional javelina use this trail. Desert wildlife abounds in this protected area, and trail riders may also see a variety of birds, including the familiar roadrunner.

30

The Arizona Trail
American Flag Trailhead

LOCATION: Northeast of Tucson and southeast of Phoenix near Oracle, Arizona. Ten miles east of Oracle Junction on State Route 77 to Globe.

LENGTH: 7-mile loop trail

COUNTY: Pinal

USE: Very light

SEASON: Almost year round

RATING: Moderate to Difficult

ELEVATION: 4,300' to 6,000'

USGS TOPO MAP: Oracle SE, Campo Bonito

CONTACT AGENCY: Coronado National Forest, Santa Catalina Ranger District

HORSE TRAILER PARKING: At the American Flag Trailhead there is enough room for 5-6 horse trailers in wide pulloffs on both sides of the road. If a group wants to ride the trail, there is ample parking at the YMCA camp on the road 1/2 mile ahead, with a connecting trail leading to the Arizona Trail from the parking area. A fee is charged for parking at the YMCA camp. Prior arrangements must be made with the YMCA; call (520-884-0987).

WATER FOR HORSES: Seasonal water may be available at Twin Ponds, 3/4 mile from the trailhead on Cody Trail. There is no reliable water at the American Flag Trailhead at the present time. Bring water with you.

CORRALS: There are two large wooden corrals and a loading chute right beside the trailhead. The corrals are privately owned and may be in use and unavailable.

OTHER FACILITIES: One mile up the trail is High Jinks Ranch, which is listed on the National Register of Historic Places. Dean Prichard, the steward for this portion of the Arizona Trail, lives there. The ranch may be visited by special arrangement by calling 520-896-2005.

ACCESS: Travel north from Tucson on Oracle Road, State Route 77, to Oracle Junction. Pass the intersection of State Route 79 from Florence, continue on Route 77, past the entrance to Biosphere 2, to

(Continued)

The Arizona Trail
American Flag Trailhead

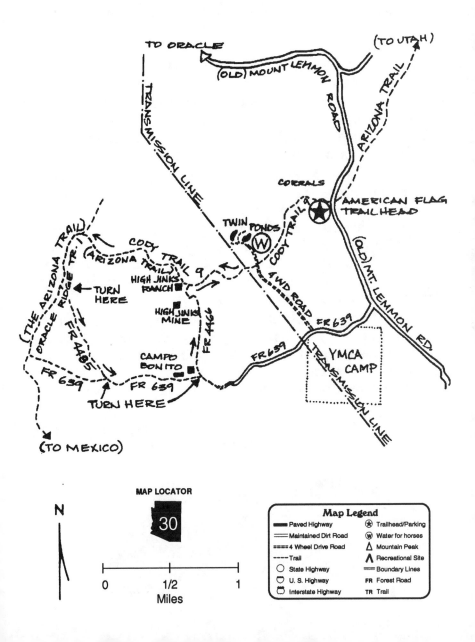

mile marker 100. Turn south (right) into the Oracle business district. Continue on the main road until it splits at the east end of town. Take the south (right) fork, which is the (Old) Mount Lemmon Road (also called the Control Road and FR 38). Travel 4 miles on this paved road, which turns into a well-maintained dirt road and turn right again when the road forks. Within .25 mile the American Flag Trailhead will appear on the right side of the road, just past the wooden corrals. A tall wooden entrance sign inscribed with the words "The Arizona Trail" frames the trailhead.

DESCRIPTION: William F. "Buffalo Bill" Cody roamed this area in the early 1900's when there was mining activity at Campo Bonito, which was a very large encampment with several families and their dwellings. They mined and processed ores from the hills in the surrounding area. Much of the trail on this loop was ridden by Buffalo Bill and it is known locally as the Cody Trail.

The Cody Trail #9 begins to climb immediately as you pass beneath The Arizona Trail sign on the west side of the road. The trail then drops into a creek bottom lush with typical Arizona riparian plants and birds. At approximately 1/2 mile from the trailhead you will cross a 4WD primitive road. You can make a right turn here and go several hundred yards down the road to Twin Ponds where you can water your horse if seasonal water is available. *There is no other dependable water on the rest of this loop.*

Return to the Cody (Arizona) Trail. Watch for the trail marker on your right as it is easy to miss. Turn right, and the trail begins to climb again. It makes a sharp right turn to go around High Jinks Ranch, then winds its way across beautiful high desert vegetation slopes. The trail passes a large outcropping of milk quartz that looks ghost-like in the distance.

Eventually the trail reaches the Oracle Ridge Trail #1 at a summit and a fence line, providing a vista of Picacho Peak in the

(Continued)

distance and Biosphere 2 just below. Here the Cody Trail ends and you turn south (left) to continue the loop on the Oracle Ridge Trail as it parallels the fence line. In approximately .25 mile you reach FR 4485 and a sign indicating the trail to Campo Bonito. At this point you leave the Arizona Trail and turn southeast (left) on FR 4485 which will take you to FR 639 and on to Campo Bonito and back to the American Flag Trailhead. (See map.)

Although this 7 mile loop ride leaves the Arizona Trail, it is an interesting route, taking you right through the original site of the Campo Bonito mining camp. Some of the building foundations are so overgrown with trees and shrubs they are hard to see. When FR 639 meets a dirt passenger vehicle road (FR 4466), make a very sharp left turn and go up the hill to the entrance of High Jinks Ranch on the left. As you pass the ranch entrance, you will see a trail straight ahead and a directional sign for The Arizona Trail. Take this trail and it will connect back to the Cody Trail. Turn right on the Cody Trail and return to the American Flag Trailhead by following the signs.

NOTE: If you continued on the Oracle Ridge/Arizona Trail, you would climb another 500 feet to skirt by Apache Peak, the large, pointed mountain that predominates the southern skyline. From there the Arizona Trail follows Oracle Ridge to the top of the Santa Catalina Mountains and continues on to eventually end at the Arizona/Mexico border.

Superstition Wilderness Trails

LOCATION: East of Phoenix near Apache Junction. North of U.S. Highway 60 to Florence Junction.

LENGTH: 8.2 mile loop ride.　**COUNTY:** Pinal and Maricopa

USE: Moderate to Heavy　**SEASON:** Oct. through May

RATING: Difficult to Very Difficult **ELEVATION:** 1,300' to 2,300'

USGS TOPO MAP: Goldfield, Weaver's Needle

CONTACT AGENCY: Tonto National Forest, Mesa Ranger District

HORSE TRAILER PARKING: Ample pull-through trailer parking and metal hitching posts at equestrian staging areas at First Water and Peralta Trailheads. Day parking fees may be charged.

WATER FOR HORSES: None at trailheads and no dependable water on most of the trails. However, if there has been any recent rain, there may be some water in the stream beds and rock pools along the trail. Several springs are in the vicinity of the canyons, and cottonwood trees grow where the springs are, so look for the cottonwoods for a possible place to water your horse.

CORRALS: None at trailheads. There are corrals at locations for overnight pack trips at Reavis Ranch, Bluff Spring, and Angel Springs. These barbed wire roundup-type corrals are large and open.

OTHER FACILITIES: Comfort station at Peralta Trailhead only. Hitching posts at First Water and Peralta Trailheads in the equestrian staging areas. Overnight camping is permitted in the areas around the hitching posts.

ACCESS: Travel east on U.S. Highway 60 from Phoenix toward Apache Junction. Take Exit 196, Idaho Road, to State Route 88 and travel north 1 mile; turn right onto State Route 88. Travel east 3.5 miles to the road to First Water Trailhead right after mile marker 200. Turn right (east) on the bumpy but passable dirt road, FR 78

(Continued)

Superstition Wilderness Trails

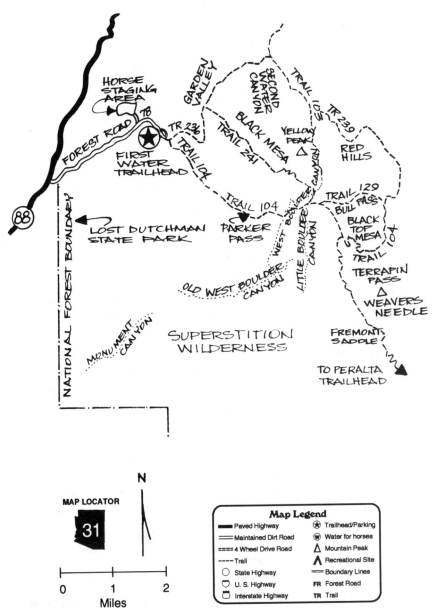

HORSE STAGING AREA

FOREST ROAD 78

FIRST WATER TRAILHEAD

TRAIL 104

TR 236

GARDEN VALLEY

SECOND WATER CANYON

BLACK MESA

TRAIL 241

TRAIL 103

TR 239

YELLOW PEAK

RED HILLS

TRAIL 129

BULL PASS

TRAIL 104

PARKER PASS

WEST BOULDER CANYON

LITTLE BOULDER CANYON

BLACK TOP MESA

TRAIL 104

TERRAPIN PASS

WEAVERS NEEDLE

LOST DUTCHMAN STATE PARK

88

NATIONAL FOREST BOUNDARY

OLD WEST BOULDER CANYON

MONUMENT CANYON

SUPERSTITION WILDERNESS

FREMONT SADDLE

TO PERALTA TRAILHEAD

MAP LOCATOR

31

N

0   1   2
Miles

Map Legend

▬ Paved Highway	⊛ Trailhead/Parking
═ Maintained Dirt Road	ⓦ Water for horses
═══ 4 Wheel Drive Road	△ Mountain Peak
---- Trail	⋀ Recreational Site
○ State Highway	═══ Boundary Lines
⬭ U. S. Highway	FR Forest Road
⬗ Interstate Highway	TR Trail

and travel approximately 3 miles to the large equestrian staging area on the north side of the road. It has two long metal hitching posts.

To get to the trailhead entrance in the wilderness area, take the .25 mile connecting trail at the east end of the parking area. It immediately crosses and parallels the road on the south.

The Peralta Trailhead is further east on U.S. Highway 60. *The trails on the south side of the Superstitions are so rugged that they're not included in this publication. It is suggested that you go into this area only with an experienced guide.*

From U.S. Highway 60, between mile markers 19 and 20 on the north side of the highway, turn north on Peralta Road (FR 77). At 6 miles the road forks; take the left fork and continue 1.8 miles to the large equestrian staging area. Make a tight left turn off the road at the sign for bus parking. One long metal hitching post is in this large parking area. The Peralta Trailhead is just down the road 0.2 mile from the staging area.

DESCRIPTION: A vast 180-mile network of trails exists throughout the Superstition Mountains and all trails are typical of the rugged terrain found in this distinctive mountain range.

The trails are well-developed and heavily used by hikers, but the area is so large that you rarely see anyone. Most of the trails are signed at intersections.

One suggested day ride is the Dutchman's Trail #104, which begins at First Water Trailhead and goes through Parker Pass to Boulder Basin. You can return on this trail or ride a loop by starting out at Second Water Trail #236, turning east on Black Mesa Trail #241, and completing the 9.1 mile loop by ending on the Dutchman's Trail #104. On this loop beginning on trail #236 you will go through Garden Valley where old remains of Spanish dwellings are found. In several areas the canyons open up and you'll see wonderful views of Weaver's Needle, the distinctive monolith that dominates the skyline. You will pass Palomino Mountain, the large yellow-orange, rock-topped mountain southeast of the trail (look for the horse's head shape in rocks up on the top). The climb up to Black Mesa, Trail #241, is a 1,000 foot ascent and the cholla cactus "forest" on top of the mesa is unbelievably dense. *Only well-conditioned trail horses should attempt this very strenuous, slick-rocks trail.*

Florida Canyon Trail

LOCATION: On the slopes of Mt. Wrightson. Between Tucson and Nogales near Green Valley. Approx. 10 miles east of Interstate 19.

LENGTH: Florida Saddle 4.6 mi.   **COUNTY:** Pima and Santa Cruz

USE: Light to Moderate   **SEASON:** April through Nov.

RATING: Very difficult   **ELEVATION:** 4,300' to 7,800'

CONTACT AGENCY: Coronado National Forest, Nogales Ranger District.

USGS TOPO MAP: Mt. Wrightson, Helvetia

WATER FOR HORSES: No dependable water at the trailhead or on the trails. There is a creek that only has water seasonally. On the trail are several water troughs for cattle that usually have water in them.

CORRALS: None

OTHER FACILITIES: None. Past the trailhead is the headquarters for Santa Rita Experimental Range administered by the University of Arizona College of Agriculture. The facilities may be utilized by special arrangement, advance reservation and the payment of a small use-fee by calling 602-625-2121.

ACCESS: From Interstate 10 in Tucson take Interstate Exit 260 south on Interstate 19 toward Nogales. Travel approximately 25 miles to the Continental Road Exit 63, near Green Valley. Turn east (left), following the signs to Madera Canyon. Go over the Santa Cruz River bridge, turn right at White House Canyon Road, follow a sharp left curve to head east and begin the climb toward Madera Canyon. Travel approximately 7.3 miles until you reach FR 62, a dirt road that turns left off the paved road to Madera Canyon. Drive 0.3 mile, cross over a cattle guard and take the right fork onto FR 62A. Continue another 3.3 miles on a good dirt road to the trailhead near the entrance to the University of Arizona Experimental Range Headquarters.

DESCRIPTION: Florida (Spanish pronunciation Flo-ree'-dah, meaning "flowered") Canyon is well-named because the canyon has

(Continued)

Florida Canyon Trail

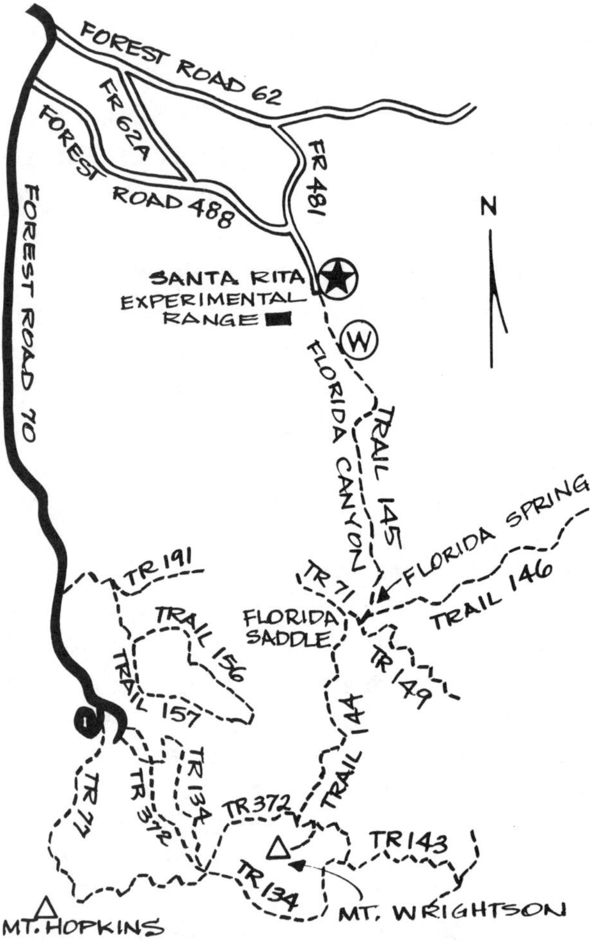

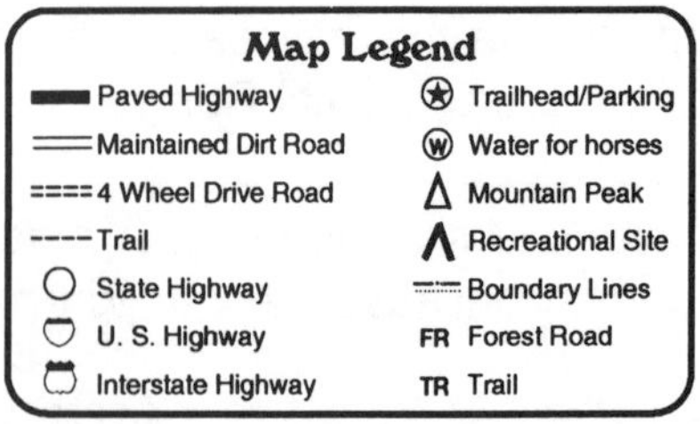

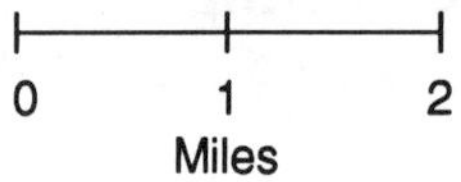

abundant flowers near the springs that seep along the trail.

In the 1880's there were 100-foot copper mine tunnels and shallow shafts near where the trail is now. The mining camp and spring were named after Charles Robinson, the owner of the mining claim. The mining operations lasted only 20 years.

The Florida Canyon Trail #145 is primarily within the Mt. Wrightson Wilderness, so only hikers and equestrians utilize this trail. The trail is well-defined and signed. It gains elevation steadily, at about the rate of 1,000 feet per mile, but it has the advantage of being much less crowded than the Madera Canyon trails and reaches the same areas of the Santa Rita mountain range.

Along the trail the views of the valley are magnificent. In the higher portions of the trail are tall Arizona sycamore trees, wild grape vines, and a canopy of oak and fir trees. Cardinals and other birds abound. Some raccoons or coatimundi may be in the grapevine area because this is a favorite foraging area. The trail frequently passes a partially buried water pipe and eventually descends toward a grassy area that usually has flowers; this is Florida Spring.

As you near the head of the canyon, the trail becomes exceptionally pretty as it goes along under tall Douglas fir and ponderosa pines which provide a canopy of shade. Florida Saddle is a perfect place for a rest break or overnight camp. There is a trail junction at Florida Saddle. The Crest Trail #144 connects the Old Baldy Trail #372 and the Super Trail #134 to the summit of Mt. Wrightson.

*A curious character, the
coatimundi!*

Juan Bautista de Anza National Historic Trail

LOCATION: 45 miles south of Tucson on Interstate 19 between the Tubac Presidio State Historic Park and Tumacacori National Historic Park.

LENGTH: 4.5 miles one way

USE: Moderate

RATING: Easy to Moderate

USGS TOPO MAP: Tubac

COUNTY: Santa Cruz

SEASON: Sept. through May

ELEVATION: 3,400'

CONTACT AGENCY: Tubac Presidio State Historic Park or The Anza Trail Coalition of Arizona (520-398-2252)

HORSE TRAILER PARKING: There is very limited (almost none) parking at the northern trailhead at Tubac. It would be best to locate a parking place along Calle Baca Road by turning north off Plaza Road as you enter the shopping area from the freeway access road. Calle Baca Road ends in several blocks at a baseball park where there is room for horse trailer turn-around.

The parking is much better at the southern Tumacacori trailhead, located 4 miles south of the Tubac Presidio. Drive north of the Tumacacori Mission and park by the trailhead. This is a large, easy access, pull-through and turn-around area for horse trailers.

WATER FOR HORSES: The Anza Trail twice crosses the Santa Cruz River, which always has water in it.

CORRALS: None for public use

OTHER FACILITIES: Restrooms and drinking water at Information Centers.

ACCESS: Travel on Interstate 10 to Tucson and take Exit 260 south of Tucson on Interstate 19 toward Nogales. Travel approximately 45 miles to Exit 34 at Tubac or 50 miles to Tumacacori Exit 29. Turn east (left) and pass under the interstate highway. Turn north (left) on the access road for either location. Turn east (right) at the Tubac entrance. A series of shops continue for several blocks

(Continued)

Juan Bautista de Anza National Historic Trail

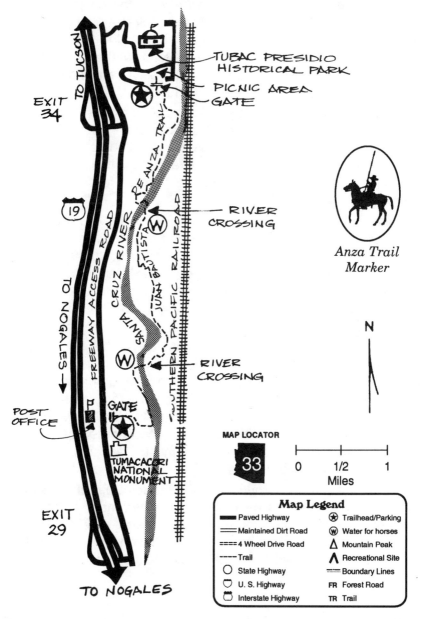

TO TUCSON

EXIT 34

19

TO NOGALES →

POST OFFICE

EXIT 29

FREEWAY ACCESS ROAD

SANTA CRUZ RIVER

JUAN BAUTISTA DE ANZA TRAIL

SOUTHERN PACIFIC RAILROAD

TUBAC PRESIDIO HISTORICAL PARK

PICNIC AREA

GATE

RIVER CROSSING

RIVER CROSSING

GATE

TUMACACORI NATIONAL MONUMENT

TO NOGALES

Anza Trail Marker

N

MAP LOCATOR

33

| 0 | 1/2 | 1 |

Miles

Map Legend

■■ Paved Highway	⊛ Trailhead/Parking
═══ Maintained Dirt Road	ⓦ Water for horses
==== 4 Wheel Drive Road	Δ Mountain Peak
---- Trail	Λ Recreational Site
◯ State Highway	⚬⚬⚬ Boundary Lines
⬡ U. S. Highway	FR Forest Road
⬒ Interstate Highway	TR Trail

before the Presidio and trailhead. The trailhead is near the Presidio Information Center, which is east of the shops and church. The trail starts at the south end of the picnic area across the street from the Presidio Information Center. A gate and signage are right at the fence line.

If you choose to start at the southern trailhead, the access is much better. To reach this trailhead continue on Interstate 19 to Exit 29 and turn north on the access road following the signs to the Tumacacori Mission. The trailhead is several hundred yards north of the Mission, across from the Post Office. A swinging gate for equestrians and a hiker's gate lead to the trail.

DESCRIPTION: Juan Bautista de Anza was one of the commanding officers of the troops that were stationed at the Tubac Presidio during Indian uprisings. His fame is attributed to an historic trailblazing trip from Nogales to San Francisco with 50 men in his company. Many of the roads in existence today follow the same route he established.

The Tumacacori to Tubac portions of this historic trail have been maintained and signage has been established by the Anza Trail Coalition, a non-profit association dedicated to the maintenance and reestablishment of this trail on public lands. It crosses through private lands, but is open to the public as a result of access agreements between the owners and the Anza Trail Coalition of Arizona.

Only equestrians and hikers are permitted on this trail section which is in the riparian fringe of the Santa Cruz River. It crosses the river two times and meanders through cottonwood groves, mesquite bosque and open fields filled with sunflowers in late summer, and myriads of wildflowers in the spring. The trail is a bird watcher's paradise. Deer, javelina, coatimundi and raccoons also abound on the trail. The trail is very soft and sandy most of the route and quite sandy in the areas close to the river.

The trail passes through the Center for Spanish Colonial Archaeology and several early Native American sites. Archaeologists can frequently be seen at digs in the area near the Tubac trailhead. Mount Hopkins and Mount Wrightson are visible to the east and the Tumacacori mountain range to the west.

MAP LOCATOR

The Arizona Trail
Canelo Pass Trailhead

LOCATION: Southeast of Tucson, near Sonoita, and State Route 83 to Parker Canyon Lake.

LENGTH: 14 miles one way **COUNTY:** Santa Cruz

USE: Light **SEASON:** April through Nov.

RATING: Moderate **ELEVATION:** 5,320' to 5,800'

CONTACT AGENCY: Coronado National Forest, Sierra Vista Ranger District

USGS TOPO MAP: O'Donnell Canyon, Canelo Pass, and Huachuca Peak

HORSE TRAILER PARKING: Loop turn-around parking at the Canelo Pass Trailhead with space for 4-6 horse trailers. Additional parking space for 2-3 horse trailers is available at the turnoff to the trailhead along the roadside. A trailhead is scheduled to be built at Canelo Pass in 1994.

WATER FOR HORSES: None available at trailhead. There is no dependable water source until you reach Parker Canyon Lake.

CORRALS: None

OTHER FACILITIES: None

ACCESS: Travel east from Tucson on Interstate 10 toward Benson. Take Exit 281 south (right) to Sonoita on State Route 83. Travel south 25 miles to the intersection of State Route 82 to Patagonia at mile marker 32.3. Go straight through this intersection, staying on State Route 83 and follow the road as it curves to the east (left) to Parker Canyon Lake. The paved road makes a sharp right turn at the junction of Elgin Road at mile marker 29.3. Stay on the paved road. At mile marker 21 you will enter the Coronado National Forest. The paved road ends and becomes a well-maintained dirt road. At the junction of State Route 83 and FR 799, go straight on FR 799 3.5 miles to the Arizona Trail trailhead. Turn west (right) and drive 100 yards on the dirt road into the parking area.

(Continued)

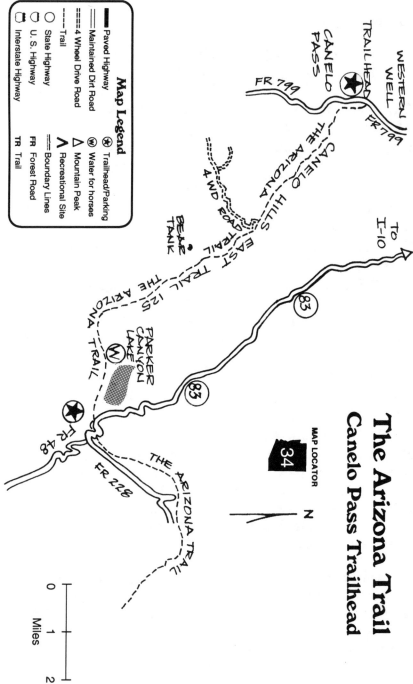

The Arizona Trail
Canelo Pass Trailhead

Map Legend

▬ Paved Highway	★ Trailhead/Parking
══ Maintained Dirt Road	Ⓦ Water for horses
════ 4 Wheel Drive Road	△ Mountain Peak
----- Trail	▲ Recreational Site
○ State Highway	▭ Boundary Lines
◌ U. S. Highway	FR Forest Road
▢ Interstate Highway	TR Trail

MAP LOCATOR

34

N

DESCRIPTION: The Arizona Trail winds between Mexico and Utah. This section, between Canelo Pass and Parker Canyon Lake, was completed and dedicated in June 1993. At the time of publication, signage on the northern section of the Arizona Trail to Harshaw Canyon, near Patagonia, had not been completed. It is expected that this portion will be signed and well established by late-1998.

Canelo Hills East Trail #125 climbs through manzanita and oak to the top of a ridge that provides excellent views of the Huachuca Mountains to the east and Santa Cruz River Valley and Patagonia Mountains to the west. Some long climbs up and down occur on this trail, but it is not extremely difficult nor strenuous if you give your horse frequent rest stops.

There are some rocky sections, and the trail will drop down into canyons and circle around ridges as it heads toward Parker Canyon Lake. The 14 miles to Parker Canyon Lake make this a difficult trail to ride in one day. However, you can divide up into two groups. One can start at Parker Canyon Lake Trailhead and the other at Canelo Pass Trailhead and exchange vehicle keys midway or, arrange a shuttle. Parker Canyon Lake is 12 miles by road from the Canelo Pass Trailhead. If you want a shorter ride, just ride the trail as far as you desire, turn around, and enjoy the views of Mt. Wrightson, the Rincons, and Mt. Lemmon. This section of the trail makes a nice overnight trip.

Packin' in along the Arizona Trail

35

General Crook Trail
Copper Canyon Segment

LOCATION: 66 miles north of Bell Road in Phoenix, just off Interstate 17 before Camp Verde. Yavapai County.

LENGTH: 5.8 miles one way   **COUNTY:** Yavapai

USE: Light   **SEASON:** Sept. through May

RATING: Moderate   **ELEVATION:** 3,800' to 4,400'

USGS TOPO MAP: Middle Verde

CONTACT AGENCY: Prescott National Forest, Verde Ranger District

HORSE TRAILER PARKING: Wide pulloff areas at the dirt road that accesses the trail, with room to pull through to turn around.

WATER FOR HORSES: There is a windmill 1/4 mile from the parking area with a large water trough, and there is dependable water in Copper Creek which flows through Copper Canyon, and is accessible from the trail.

CORRALS: None

OTHER FACILITIES: None

ACCESS: Travel north from Phoenix on Interstate 17 toward Flagstaff. Go past Cordes Junction and take Exit 278 at Cherry Road. Turn east (right) and travel .25 mile to a dirt road on the north (left) side of the highway. Turn on this dirt road and park off the road at a wide pulloff area. The road to San Dominique Winery is on the south (right) side across from the trail parking area.

DESCRIPTION: This trail winds its way down and into an idyllic canyon filled with trees and a stream that makes its way to the Verde River in Camp Verde. The trail is the original wagon road used by General George Crook and his troops as he patrolled for Apache Indians in the 1870's. The Indians were reluctant to enter the canyon, for unknown reasons, but they would shoot from the canyon's rim at troops and travelers going from Camp Verde to Prescott.

Copper Canyon offered the area's best shade and water

(Continued)

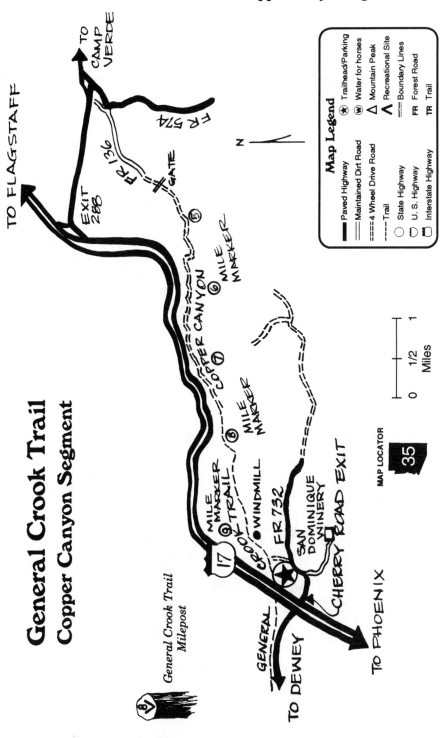

available to early travelers. Remnants of homesteads existing there are evidenced by apricot trees, other fruit and nut trees and cement foundations in a grassy clearing midway in the canyon.

To reach the trail into Copper Canyon, ride north on the dirt road over a rise and parallel Interstate 17 for 500 yards. The General Crook Trail is marked with piles of rocks encased in wire (cairns) and wooden mile markers. When you reach the General Crook Trail, you will be between mile markers V10 and V9. (The "V" represents the distance from the Fort at Camp Verde where the mile markers begin at "0".) Turn east (right) and follow the wire-encased cairns until you reach a windmill and water trough. Look for mile post V9 to the north of the windmill and you will know you are on the trail.

The trail descends and shortly after mile marker V8 there is evidence of some of the black powder blasting done in 1874 to make the wagon road into the canyon. The homestead ruins are near mile marker V7, which makes a good area for a rest break. The stream is on the north side of the trail. At some points Interstate 17 is visible along the top of the canyon. Eventually you will reach a green gate near mile marker V4. The gate is a good place to turn around and return to the trailhead as the trail ahead exits the canyon and enters the outskirts of Camp Verde.

Sharing lunch along the trail . . .

36

Granite Mountain Area Trails

LOCATION: 9 miles west of Prescott off Iron Springs Road.

LENGTH: Varies with the trail(s) **COUNTY:** Yavapai

USE: Moderate to Heavy **SEASON:** April through Nov.

RATING: Moderate **ELEVATION:** 5,600' to 5,800'

USGS TOPO MAP: Iron Springs

CONTACT AGENCY: Prescott National Forest, Bradshaw Ranger District

HORSE TRAILER PARKING: Large turn-around area for horse trailers at the Cayuse Equestrian Trailhead. Day use only.

WATER FOR HORSES: Water trough at equestrian trailhead.

OTHER FACILITIES: Comfort stations and hitching posts are available at the trailhead.

ACCESS: Travel north from Phoenix on Interstate 17 to Cordes Junction Exit 262 and follow State Route 69 into Prescott. Stay on the north (right) side of the road as you enter Prescott and follow the highway signs for Highway 89 *South*. Turn right on Sheldon Street. (It dead ends at Montezuma St. by the old, restored Santa Fe train depot.) Turn right on Montezuma and continue to the intersection of Willow Creek, Miller Valley and Iron Springs Roads. Continue straight ahead. Montezuma Street becomes Iron Springs Road. Follow this road out of town. When you reach the Williamson Valley Road intersection, check your odometer reading. (A fire station is on the right at this intersection.) Travel approximately 1.8 miles on Iron Springs Road from this intersection to Granite Basin Road (FR 374). Turn north (right) on FR 374 and travel 1.5 miles to the Cayuse Equestrian Staging Area, located on the right (east) side of the road.

DESCRIPTION: *Barry Goldwater, this area of trails is dedicated to you!* (This is the area where Senator Goldwater, statesman and presidential candidate, often enjoyed horseback outings.)

The wide assortment of recreational trails around Granite Mountain, Granite Lake, and Granite Basin are used extensively by hikers, mountain bikers, and equestrians. The best area for eques-

(Continued)

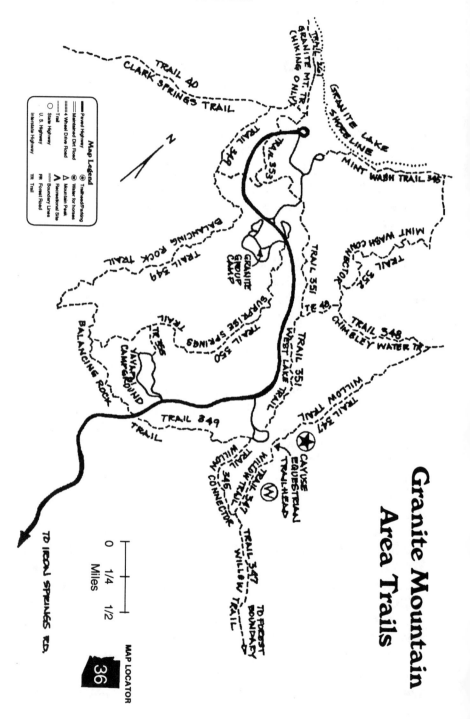

Granite Mountain
Area Trails

trians is east of Granite Lake, in the oak, juniper and pine trees. The trails are well marked and provide a number of options for hours of riding pleasure, depending upon the trails selected.

Cayuse Equestrian Trailhead has ample pull-through parking for equestrians, and it is well-planned with many areas for parking horse trailers and saddling up. It is open only for day use. Overnight camping is not allowed at this trailhead. Water for horses and public restrooms for riders help make this trailhead especially desirable.

Three trails leave the equestrian trailhead. On the north side is Westlake Trail #351, which takes riders close to Granite Lake and some of the more popular hiking and picnic areas. This trail eventually intersects Balancing Rock Trail #349, which loops back to the equestrian trailhead for an approximate 5-mile loop ride.

If you turn right off of Westlake Trail on Chimbley Water Trail #348 approximately 1 mile from the trailhead, you will reach the Mint Wash Connector Trail #352 after 300 yards. If you turn left on the Mint Wash Connector Trail, it will intersect the Mint Wash Trail #352 after 300 yards. If you turn left on the Mint Wash Connector Trail, it will intersect the Mint Wash Trail #345 in approximately 2 miles. The Mint Wash Trail ends in 1 mile at the boat launch area at Granite Lake if you turn left (southwest).

The second trail leading out of the equestrian trailhead is Balancing Rock Trail #349, which heads southwest, intersects Surprise Spring Trail #350 in one mile, Westlake Trail #351 in 2 1/2 miles, and then intersects Clark Springs Trail #40 and Granite Mountain Trail #261 in 3 miles. If you turn left on Clark Springs Trail, it ends in about 2 miles at Little Granite Mountain Trail #37 which runs south and ends at a small passenger car trailhead on Iron Springs Road.

The third trail leading out of the equestrian trailhead is Willow Connector Trail #346, at the south end of the parking area. This trail connects to the Willow Trail #347 in approximately 1/2 mile. If you turn left on the Willow Trail it heads north for 1.5 miles and meets the Chimbley Water Trail #348 on the left. You can return to the equestrian trailhead by turning left on Westlake Trail #351 at the end of Trail #348 for a short 2.5 mile loop ride. You also have the option of turning right and riding the Willow Trail south for 1.5 miles, where it exits the national forest boundary.

There are other trails in the Granite Basin area that head down into the lower elevations toward Contreras Road. Contact the Bradshaw Ranger District for additional information on these trails.

Groom Creek Horse Camp Trails

LOCATION: 6 miles south of Prescott on the Senator Highway.

LENGTH: 2 to 9 mile loops   **COUNTY:** Yavapai

USE: Moderate to Heavy   **SEASON:** April through Nov.

RATING: Moderate to Difficult   **ELEVATION:** 6,000' to 7,600'

USGS TOPO MAP: Groom Creek

CONTACT AGENCY: Prescott National Forest, Bradshaw Ranger District

HORSE TRAILER PARKING: 37 pull-through campsites for horse trailers are provided in this equestrian-use only campground. A small fee per unit per day is charged. Call well ahead to make reservations, as this campground is extremely popular and fills up quickly.

WATER FOR HORSES: Many spigots are provided throughout the campground for water. Bring your own buckets, or use the common watering troughs at the campground entrance.

CORRALS: None. Picket lines are provided for tethering horses. The entire campground is enclosed with fences in case a horse gets loose.

OTHER FACILITIES: Hitching posts, picnic tables, BBQ grills, lighting, and multiple comfort stations. The campground host has rakes, shovels and dumpsters for manure.

ACCESS: From Phoenix travel Interstate 17 north to Cordes Junction Exit 262. Go west on State Route 69 to Prescott. As you enter Prescott keep to the left and stay on Gurley Steet when the highway forks. Stay in the left lane for 3/4 mile and turn south (left) at the stop light on Mt. Vernon Street. This street becomes the Senator Highway. Travel 6.6 miles, passing turnoffs to Goldwater Lake, Friendly Pines Camp, and the Groom Creek Store. The horse camp is approximately 1/2 mile south of the Groom Creek Store. The entrance is on the west (right) side of the highway. Across the

(Continued)

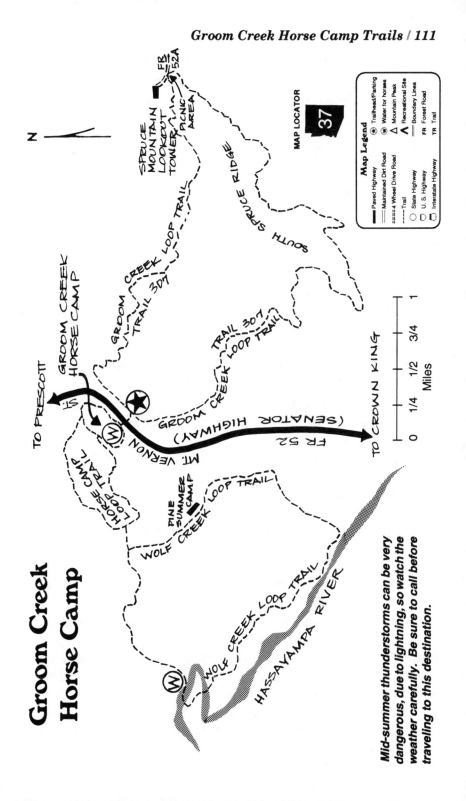

Groom Creek Horse Camp

N

TO PRESCOTT

GROOM CREEK HORSE CAMP

SPRUCE MOUNTAIN LOOKOUT TOWER

FR 52A

PICNIC AREA

GROOM CREEK LOOP TRAIL 307

SOUTH SPRUCE RIDGE

TRAIL 307

GROOM CREEK LOOP TRAIL

GROOM CREEK LOOP TRAIL

MT. VERNON (SENATOR) HIGHWAY

FR 52

TO CROWN KING

HORSE CAMP LOOP TRAIL

PINE SUMMER CAMP

WOLF CREEK LOOP TRAIL

WOLF CREEK LOOP TRAIL

HASSAYAMPA RIVER

0   1/4   1/2   3/4   1
Miles

Mid-summer thunderstorms can be very dangerous, due to lightning, so watch the weather carefully. Be sure to call before traveling to this destination.

street on the east (left) side of the highway is a pull-through parking area for horse trailers for day use of the Groom Creek Loop Trail.

DESCRIPTION: Groom Creek Horse Camp was constructed through the joint efforts of active Arizona equestrians led by Isabelle Brown, Cathy Hubbard, Vicki Muecke, Sally Allen and the U.S. Forest Service with the funding encouragement of Senator Dennis DeConcini.

The campground was built for the exclusive use of the equestrian camper and any use of the facility without a horse is prohibited. There is a nominal charge for overnight use of the campground facilities and campers are limited to the number of days at campsites. All of the campsites are reservable except for a few that are kept open for "first-come, first-served" arrivals. *Trailers over 35 feet in length are prohibited* because the campsites cannot accommodate them. Reservations are currently made through the Bradshaw Ranger District in Prescott, 602-445-7253.

There are three loop trails of varying lengths from the horse camp area. Hikers and mountain bikers are also permitted to use the trails, but the majority of users are equestrians.

The shortest loop trail is the Horse Camp Loop, 2 miles in length. This trail begins at a gate near campsite #26 and is marked with yellow flags.

The middle length loop trail is Wolf Creek Loop, 5 miles in length. This trail begins midway on the Horse Camp Loop and is marked with blue flags.

The longest loop trail is the Groom Creek Loop, 9 miles in length. The trail is designated #307 on all signage. This trailhead is across the paved road from the entrance to the horse camp and can be accessed by using a connecting trail that goes through the gate and heads south (left) outside the fence around the horse camp.

Highlights on the trails include the Hassayampa River, midway on the Wolf Creek Loop, and the Spruce Mountain lookout tower midway on the Groom Creek Trail. A hitching post, picnic table and primitive restroom located at the road entrance to the lookout tower provide a perfect place for a rest stop.

The altitudes are high, and even though the trails are well-constructed and have gradual switchback climbs, they can exhaust horses easily.

38

Red Rock/Secret Mountain Wilderness Trails

Long Canyon Trail

LOCATION: 3 miles west of town center in Sedona, 3 miles north of State Route 89A.

LENGTH: 2.9 miles one way

COUNTY: Yavapai

USE: Moderate to Heavy

SEASON: Year round

RATING: Moderate

ELEVATION: 4,400' to 5,300'

USGS TOPO MAP: Wilson Mountain

CONTACT AGENCY: Coconino National Forest, Sedona Ranger District

HORSE TRAILER PARKING: Park 0.3 mile from the trailhead on the east side of FR 152C. This parking area is located to the right of the junction of Dry Creek Road (FR 152C) and the road to Boynton Canyon. A wide sandy area (accessed by several turnouts off 152C and 152D) runs along the edges of Dry Creek. The area is large enough for many horse trailers. The actual trailhead is ahead on the paved road, but it is very small and usually filled with passenger vehicles.

WATER FOR HORSES: No dependable water source. Water will sometimes be available in Dry Creek beside the parking area.

CORRALS: None

OTHER FACILITIES: None

ACCESS: From Phoenix, travel north on Interstate 17 to Exit 298 to State Route 179 to Sedona. Exit and turn left, going back under the freeway. Travel through the Village of Oak Creek and continue to stop light in Sedona where Route 179 junctions with State Route 89A. Turn southwest (left) on State Route 89A toward Cottonwood and travel 3.2 miles to mile marker 371. Turn north (right) on Dry Creek Road, Forest Route 152C. Follow Dry Creek Road 6.1 miles to the stop sign. The paved road to the right is Long Canyon Road. (Horse trailer parking is best at this junction.) Park and unload your horse by Dry Creek. Ride north along the sandy area by Dry Creek for 0.6 mile, paralleling the paved road. Where the paved road makes a sharp turn to the left, **cross the road carefully (tour buses and jeep tours are frequent users).** Look for the trailhead (on the left) marked with a rusty metal sign "Long Canyon #122." There are large boulders blocking vehicle access to the trail.

DESCRIPTION: The trail is wonderfully soft and sandy for horses. It begins as a 4WD-type road, heading directly toward the red rock cliffs on the horizon. At 0.3 mile there will be three forks in the trail. Go left and follow the trail until it reaches a large Forest Service metal gate at 0.6 mile. The gate is the entrance into the Red Rock-Secret Mountain Wilderness Area. At 1.0 mile there is another fork. One trail goes left along a power line toward Boynton Canyon and the other goes right to Long Canyon. The Long Canyon Trail heads directly toward the white cliffs above the red rock of Maroon Mountain. After another 0.5 mile you will see cypress trees and after 2.5 miles the trees become more alpine with alligator bark juniper and oaks.

As you reach 2.9 miles on the trail it becomes very steep as it turns straight north and climbs into a side canyon where it ends. **The best place to turn around is before the trail starts this steep climb.**

You can either return to the trailhead the way you came for a short 3-hour ride, or you can return to the junction of the connecting trail to Boynton Canyon and ride that trail to extend your ride by 3-4 hours. Follow the signs from the junction. The Boynton Trail ascends to a flat mesa and drops into Boynton Can-yon, which winds its way up behind Enchantment Resort into some cooler, high country. When the trail narrows after 3.0 miles, you can turn around and return on the same trail, this time enjoying the totally different views of the red rock cliffs that were at your back on the ride into the canyons.

Indian Paintbrush

(Continued)

Red Rock/Secret Mountain Wilderness Area

Long Canyon Trail
and
Loy Canyon Trail

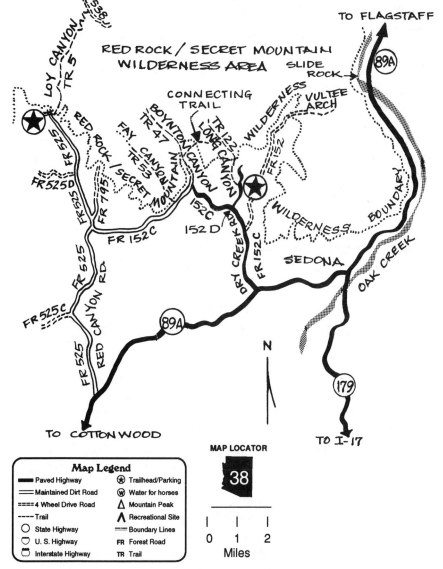

Loy Canyon Trail

LOCATION: In Sedona red rock country, off State Route 89A between Cottonwood and Sedona.

LENGTH: 5 miles   **COUNTY:** Yavapai

USE: Moderate   **SEASON:** Oct. through May

RATING: Easy to Very Difficult   **ELEVATION:** 4,270' to 6,400'

USGS TOPO MAP: Loy Butte

CONTACT AGENCY: Coconino National Forest, Sedona Ranger District

HORSE TRAILER PARKING: There is a small trailhead with a tight circle turnaround to the west (left) of the trailhead just before the cattle guard and entrance to Hancock Ranch. The trailhead has enough parking for 3-4 horse trailers unless many passenger vehicles are there. If this parking area is congested, a public easement permits vehicles to go down toward Hancock Ranch, and take the left fork (staying on FR525) to the parking area near some Indian ruins. Turn around in this area, return to the trailhead and park on the shoulder.

WATER FOR HORSES: None available at trailhead. Sometimes water is available in the creek in Loy Canyon, but this is not always dependable. Bring water for your horses when riding this trail.

CORRALS: None

ACCESS: Travel north on Interstate 17 to Flagstaff, exit at Camp Verde on Exit 287 to Cottonwood, Route 260 and Route 89A. Go west (left) to Cottonwood and travel approximately 12 miles through several stop lights to intersection of Main Street and Route 260. Turn north (right) on Route 89A to Sedona. Go approximately 10 miles until you reach mile marker 363, then slow down and watch for a dirt road on the west (left) side with a sign, a gate and a mailbox. The sign will read "Red Canyon Road" and the gate will have U.S. Fish and Game Hunt Unit 6B signage on it. FR 525 to Red Canyon is an improved gravel road. Several forks in the road will appear at 2 and 3 miles, but stay on FR 525 until you reach a fork with the sign "Loy Butte - 7 miles". Take the right fork to Loy Butte (left fork goes to Sycamore Pass on 525C). After 3 miles you will come to another junction. Stay on FR525. After 6 miles the road to Red Canyon splits off to the right on FR795. Stay on FR525. Continue past the turn to Bradshaw Road (525D) to Loy Butte, now 3 miles ahead. One mile before the trailhead, you will pass some corrals on the east (right) side of the road. The road then goes down a hill and around some curves. The trailhead parking area will appear on your left just before you cross the cattle guard and see a sign for Hancock Ranch. *It's easy to miss this trailhead, so watch carefully!*

DESCRIPTION: Loy Canyon Trail #5 follows a sandy, scenic, and well-established route with many views of the towering, windswept vermillion cliffs for which the Sedona area is renowned. The first 3 miles of the trail are very easy and fairly level. You pass by Indian cliff dwellings on the west side of the trail about 30 minutes (1/2 mile) from the trailhead. Look for the cliff dwellings high in the shadows of the overhanging cliffs. The trail is very easy to find and follow. This first 3-mile portion of the trail makes an excellent 3-4 hour ride round trip.

The last two miles of the trail are very steep, rocky and difficult. The trail climbs over 1,000 feet in one mile to the top of the ridge and ends where it meets FR538. There are many areas of sheer, broad rock on this last portion of the trail, making it hazardous for horses. If you proceed to the top, be very cautious, especially on the downhill return trip to the trailhead.

Many visitors come to see the excellent Indian ruins which are 0.4 mile from the cattle guard entrance to Hancock Ranch at the Loy Canyon trailhead. There is a parking area pulloff and turn-around on the right side of the road should you decide to visit the ruins.

Gambel Oak

West Spruce Mountain Trail

LOCATION: 3 miles southwest of Prescott on Iron Springs Road to Skull Valley and Kirkland Junction.

LENGTH: 7.4 miles one way   **COUNTY:** Yavapai

USE: Light to Moderate   **SEASON:** April through Oct.

RATING: Difficult to Very Difficult   **ELEVATION:** 5,300' to 7,100'

USGS TOPO MAP: Iron Springs

CONTACT AGENCY: Prescott National Forest, Bradshaw Ranger District

HORSE TRAILER PARKING: Limited parking with turn-around for 2-3 horse trailers in parking area beside the road at the trailhead.

WATER FOR HORSES: None at trailhead. Bring water for your horses when you ride this trail. After 25 minutes into the trail there is a small stream that usually has water in it except during dry season.

CORRALS: None

OTHER FACILITIES: None

ACCESS: Travel north from Phoenix on Interstate 17 and take Cordes Junction Exit 262 to Prescott. Stay in the right lane as you enter Prescott and turn on Sheldon Street when the road forks (Gurley Street will be the left fork). This street will dead end at Montezuma Street by the old, restored Santa Fe train depot. Turn right on Montezuma Street and continue to the intersection of Willow Creek, Miller Valley and Iron Springs Road. Make no turn, continue straight ahead. Montezuma Street becomes Iron Springs Road. Follow Iron Springs Road out of town. When you reach Williamson Valley Road, check your odometer reading. (There will be a fire station on the right at this intersection.) From this intersection travel 6.7 miles to Forest Road 43, on the southeast (left) side of the highway. (This road will be marked in three ways: Dosie Pit Road, Trail #264West Spruce Trail and 9217A.) Turn left

(Continued)

West Spruce Mountain Trail

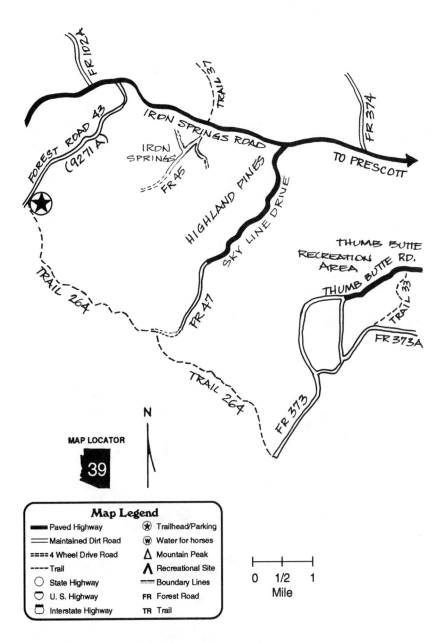

MAP LOCATOR

39

N

Map Legend

▬▬▬ Paved Highway	★ Trailhead/Parking
═══ Maintained Dirt Road	Ⓦ Water for horses
==== 4 Wheel Drive Road	△ Mountain Peak
---- Trail	∧ Recreational Site
○ State Highway	═══ Boundary Lines
▽ U. S. Highway	FR Forest Road
▣ Interstate Highway	TR Trail

0   1/2   1
Mile

on this dirt road and travel 2.3 miles to the trailhead parking area. The trail sign will be on the east (left) side of the dirt road. The parking area is on the west (right) side of the road.

DESCRIPTION: West Spruce Trail #264 weaves its way up the slopes leading to West Spruce Mountain. The climb is graded with switchbacks but still very challenging due to the long climb and higher elevations in the area. You gain 2,000 feet in elevation in the first 4 miles of the trail.

The time to ride this trail will be longer even though the distance is less than 8 miles due to the continual climb and rest stops. The trail begins in the manzanita and juniper elevations and climbs into ponderosa pines. As you make your way up toward the West Spruce Mountain summit the views of Ferguson Valley, Iron Springs and the ranches in Skull Valley are magnificent. The top of the mountain is hidden from view by the first slopes of Sugarloaf Mountain you climb. You finally see the pines at the top of the mountain 1.75 hours from the trailhead. There is a cowboy gate and fence line on the trail 2 hours into your ride. After going through the gate the trail merges with an old 4WD roadbed that goes by some mining sites and then ascends into the pine trees.

The trail terminates at FR 373, 0.5 mile north of the Sierra Prieta overlook which is approximately 4 miles from the Thumb Butte Recreation area.

West Spruce Trail #264 would be an excellent trail for conditioning endurance horses. However, it has some areas that could be challenging to your horse and uncomfortable to flat-land equestrians who do not enjoy heights. *Ride this trail with caution and a well-conditioned, trail-wise horse.*

Mountain monarchs,
Arizona's mule deer

MAP LOCATOR

Woodchute Wilderness Trail

LOCATION: Between Prescott and Jerome off of State Route 89A.

LENGTH: 5.9 miles one way   **COUNTY:** Yavapai

USE: Moderate   **SEASON:** April through Oct.

RATING: Moderate to Difficult   **ELEVATION:** 5,500' to 7,500'

USGS TOPO MAP: Hickey Mountain/Munds Draw

CONTACT AGENCY: Prescott National Forest, Verde and Chino Valley Ranger Districts.

HORSE TRAILER PARKING: Circular drive trailhead with pull-outs and wide areas for 5-6 horse trailers, gravel surface.

WATER FOR HORSES: None at trailhead. Bring water with you for horses.

CORRALS: None.

OTHER FACILITIES: Comfort station at trailhead.

ACCESS: From Phoenix travel north on Interstate 17 to Cordes Junction. Take Exit 262 at Cordes Junction and travel west on State Route 69 toward Prescott. Travel 32 miles to Prescott Valley. After mile marker 287 turn north (right) at Robert Road. Travel approximately 3 miles through Prescott Valley until road ends at Route 89A. Turn east (right) and travel 14 miles to Potato Patch Campground turnoff just beyond mile marker 335 on the west (left) side of the highway. Travel 0.3 mile and turn south (left) at entrance to Woodchute Trail parking area which is a good gravel road several hundred yards from the paved road. Park outside the gate for day use, or drive to a campsite just inside the gate if staying overnight. The trailhead to Woodchute Trail #102 is approximately .5 mile from the parking area and is reached by riding the 4WD road beyond the gate at the parking area. The road passes by a man-made water catchment tank, but it is fenced off and has no access.

DESCRIPTION: The Woodchute Wilderness is atop a high mesa overlooking the Verde, Chino, and Lonesome Valleys and distant

(Continued)

Woodchute Wilderness Trail

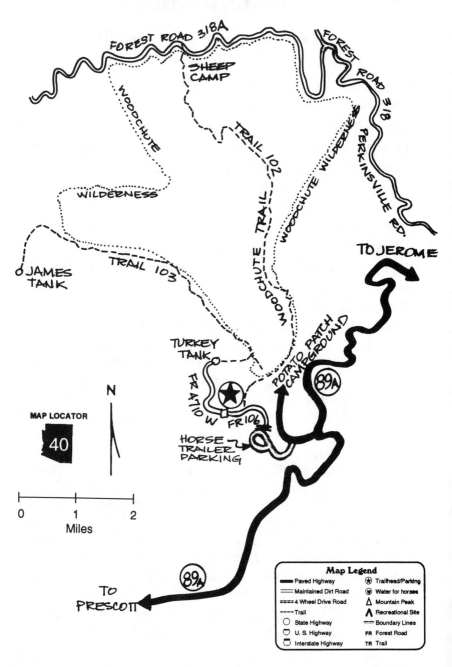

mountain ranges. Hiking and horseback riding only are allowed on the wilderness trails in this area.

Woodchute Trail #102 travels northward and ends at FR 318A at Sheep Camp, which is approximately 1.3 miles from FR 318 (Perkinsville Road) that connects Jerome and Perkinsville.

The trail passes through pine forest areas that have been left in a natural state for a true wilderness experience. At the lower elevations you will see juniper, oak and manzanita. High desert plants inhabit the north end of the trail. The top of the mountain has an open stand of second growth ponderosa pine. The original forest was completely cut many years ago when the copper mines at Jerome were in operation. Loggers obtained shoring timbers for the mines from this mountain. They transported the logs by way of a chute extending down the north side of the mountain (hence its name) to the loading platforms of the narrow gauge railroad which served Jerome. That rail bed is now FR 318.

This is not a loop trail. The roads at either end could serve as trailheads to make this a good shuttle trip for riders using this trail. It also could provide an excellent overnight experience for equestrians, if desired. There are splendid panoramic views from the mountaintop in all directions, adding to the pleasure of riding this trail.

Woodchute Mountain is over 7,500' in elevation, so be prepared for weather changes which could bring extremely cold conditions.

Watch for historic tree blazes which can be found along this trail.

Yeager Canyon Loop Trails

LOCATION: 24 miles east of Prescott on State Route 89A to Jerome and Sedona.

LENGTH: 5.7 miles round trip   **COUNTY:** Yavapai

USE: Moderate   **SEASON:** April through Oct.

RATING: Difficult   **ELEVATION:** 6,000' to 7,400'

USGS TOPO MAP: Hickey Mountain

CONTACT AGENCY: Prescott National Forest, Verde Ranger District

HORSE TRAILER PARKING: The trailhead is on the south side of the Route 89A and down a sharp, angled right turn on a dirt road. Depending upon the size of your horse trailer, this sharp angle may be a problem. It would be best if you went past the trailhead and turned around on the wide, gravel pullout on the highway 0.1 mile north of this dirt road. This approach will put you at a better angle coming in on the trailhead road.

Also, there are some unusual angles in the trailhead parking area and longer horse trailers may have difficulty maneuvering in and out. Approach the open parking areas with caution.

WATER FOR HORSES: Bring your own water. There is no reliable water source on this trail system. Sometimes there is water in the canyon from Yeager Spring or Young Seep and there is a trick tank just east of the junction of Trail #28 and #111 that may have water in it. There is a fenced wildlife watering device 2 miles from the trailhead where the trail meets FR 413 that may be accessible.

CORRALS: None

OTHER FACILITIES: None

ACCESS: Travel north out of Phoenix on Interstate 17 and take Exit 262 at Cordes Junction. Curve west (left) over the freeway and travel 27 miles to Prescott Valley on State Route 69. After mile

(Continued)

Yeager Canyon Loop Trails

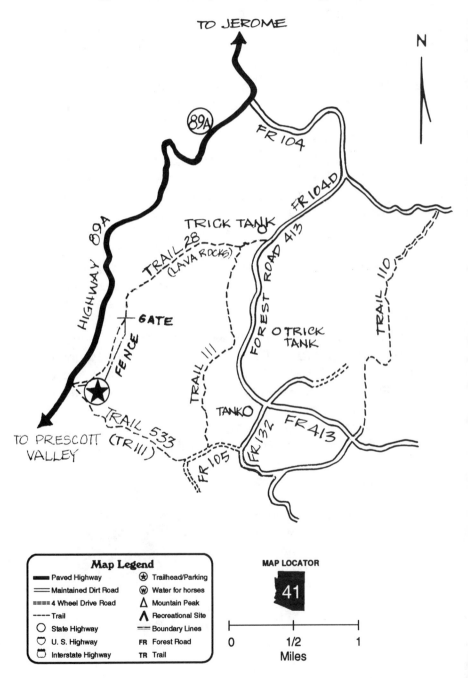

TO JEROME

N

89A

FR 104

HIGHWAY 89A

TRICK TANK

FR 104D

TRAIL 28 (LAVA ROCKS)

FOREST ROAD 413

TRAIL 110

GATE

FENCE

TRAIL 111

O TRICK TANK

TRAIL 533 (TR 111)

TANK O

FR 132   FR 413

TO PRESCOTT VALLEY

FR 105

Map Legend

▬▬ Paved Highway	✪ Trailhead/Parking
▭ Maintained Dirt Road	Ⓦ Water for horses
==== 4 Wheel Drive Road	△ Mountain Peak
---- Trail	⋀ Recreational Site
○ State Highway	Boundary Lines
♡ U. S. Highway	**FR** Forest Road
♙ Interstate Highway	**TR** Trail

MAP LOCATOR

41

0   1/2   1
Miles

marker 287 watch for the Robert Road intersection and turn north (right). Follow Robert Road approximately 3 miles through Lonesome Valley until it ends at Route 89A. Turn east (right) on Route 89A and travel approximately 9 miles to mile marker 331.5 where you enter the Prescott National Forest. The Yeager Canyon trailhead is on the south (right) side of Route 89A between mile markers 333 and 334.

DESCRIPTION: The elevation of these trails provides good riding temperatures through the spring, summer and fall, and the views of Prescott Valley, the Bradshaw Mountains, and Granite Mountain are excellent from the trails.

There are three trails that connect to form a nice loop ride into Yeager Canyon. The total distance of the loop is 5.7 miles. The trails meander through oak and pine forests most of the way, climbing 1,400 feet in elevation.

Begin on Trail #28, Yeager Canyon Trail. This trail is more steep and rocky than the others and easier to climb than descend. To reach this trail, follow the connecting trail that begins at the first cattleguard on the entrance road to the trailhead. The connecting trail parallels Route 89A. Stay to the left of the fence line and follow the trail along the edge of the canyon streambed. In 0.4 mile the connecting trail will reach Trail #28, where you cross the fence line and begin climbing to reach Trail #111 on top of Mingus Mountain. Toward the end of Trail #28 there is a volcanic rock section approximately 1/2 mile in length. Be very cautious in this area, as there are many loose rocks on the trail.

When the trail intersects the Yeager Cabin Trail #111 you will turn to the south (right). This trail section of the loop ride is 1.8 miles in length. Trail #111 will end at FR 105. Turn west (right) and follow FR 105 for 0.2 mile, until you reach Trail #533 on the northwest (right) side of FR105. The last portion of the loop is 1.9 miles back down to the trailhead parking area. When you have completed the loop you will have traveled 5.7 miles in a clockwise direction.

Pinyon Pine

Kofa Queen Trail

LOCATION: Approximately 18 miles south of Quartzsite and Interstate 10 on U.S. Highway 95 in the Kofa National Wildlife Refuge.

LENGTH: 4 miles one way   **COUNTY:** Yuma County

USE: Light   **SEASON:** Oct. through April

RATING: Moderate   **ELEVATION:** 1,900' - 2,400'

USGS TOPO MAP: Livingston Hills, Palm Canyon

CONTACT AGENCY: Kofa National Wildlife Refuge

HORSE TRAILER PARKING: Adequate shoulder parking all along the maintained dirt road leading into Kofa Queen Canyon area. No designated trailhead.

WATER FOR HORSES: No dependable water source. There are fenced water tanks for the bighorn sheep. Equestrians may use buckets to obtain water for their horses.

OTHER FACILITIES: None

ACCESS: Travel west of Phoenix on Interstate 10 to Quartzsite. Take Exit 19 and turn south on U.S. Highway 95 to Yuma. Travel approximately 18 miles and turn left (east) on the Palm Canyon Road which is between mile markers 85 and 86. At approximately 4.5 miles the road to Kofa Queen Canyon forks to the left (north). Turn on this road and travel approximately 4 more miles until you reach the mouth of the canyon at the base of Signal Peak, a 3,800' rock mountain that rises like a crown off the desert floor. Park well off the road to give adequate clearance for the roadway.

DESCRIPTION: In the early 1900's a number of mines were established in the mountainous areas of the Kofa National Wildlife Refuge. One of the most notable was the King of Arizona Mine. It gave the Kofa Mountains their name, "Kofa" being contracted from "King of Arizona." The Kofa Queen Canyon lies along the northern base of Signal Peak and follows an easterly route into the heart of the Kofa Mountains.

(Continued)

Kofa Queen Trail

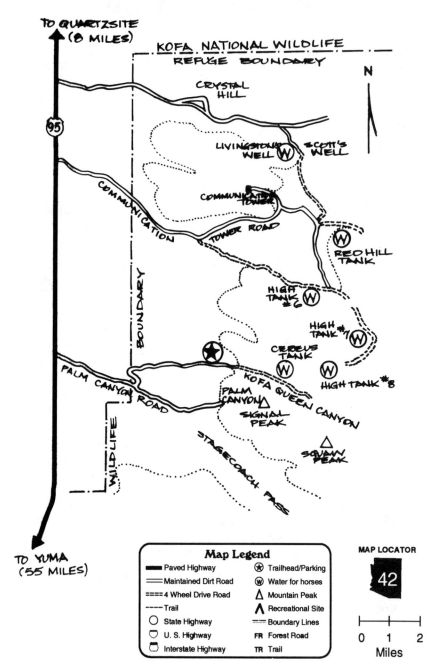

TO QUARTZSITE
(8 MILES)

KOFA NATIONAL WILDLIFE
REFUGE BOUNDARY

N

CRYSTAL HILL

95

LIVINGSTON WELL — SCOTT'S WELL

COMMUNICATION TOWER

COMMUNICATION TOWER ROAD

RED HILL TANK

HIGH TANK #6

HIGH TANK #7

BOUNDARY

PALM CANYON ROAD

CEREUS TANK

HIGH TANK #8

KOFA QUEEN CANYON

PALM CANYON

SIGNAL PEAK

WILDLIFE

STAGECOACH PASS

SQUAW PEAK

TO YUMA
(55 MILES)

Map Legend

▬ Paved Highway	✪ Trailhead/Parking
═ Maintained Dirt Road	Ⓦ Water for horses
╪ 4 Wheel Drive Road	△ Mountain Peak
--- Trail	Λ Recreational Site
○ State Highway	⦚ Boundary Lines
⬭ U. S. Highway	FR Forest Road
⬚ Interstate Highway	TR Trail

MAP LOCATOR

42

0   1   2
Miles

The entire area is part of the refuge encompassing 660,000 acres of pristine desert environment which is the home of the unique desert bighorn sheep, desert tortoise, kit foxes and the California fan palm in Palm Canyon, the only native palm in Arizona. Look for the Kofa Mountain barberry bush (leaves are very similar to holly) that can be found only in southwestern Arizona.

Citizen groups, U.S. Fish and Wildlife Service, and the Desert Bighorn Sheep Society have all worked together to enlarge natural

water holes to provide wildlife a more reliable water source. Approximately 1,000 bighorn sheep now live in the refuge. On early morning rides, you will usually see the sheep on the sides and cliffs of the canyon.

The Kofa Queen Canyon trail is a 4WD rough road that provides access into the canyon wilderness area. The roads in the wilderness area are unmaintained trails for the most part and only foot or horseback travel is permitted in the areas bordering these trails. The roads are not well signed or numbered.

Within the first mile of your ride on the canyon floor, the walls of the canyon will rise to over 3,500', and there are several natural arches on either side. At approximately 4 miles, the original site of the Kofa Queen Mine will be on the south (right) side of the canyon. The mine makes a good turn-around point on this ride. The return route is the same, but with very different perspective views of the canyon.

You may want to visit Palm Canyon while you are in the area. The trail is not suitable for horses, but there is turn-around parking at the Palm Canyon Trailhead, which is 9 miles from Highway 95.

HELP!

(Whom to call in case of an emergency)

When you have a **road emergency**, call the Arizona Highway Patrol by dialing "911" for the referral network or call the appropriate number below.

ARIZONA HIGHWAY PATROL

(Main number for all locations)
Phoenix (Central) 602-223-2000
Tucson (Southern) 520-746-4500
Flagstaff (Northern) 520-773-3700

Medical or any emergency, call the County Sheriff's Office where you are located. They will also provide the names of **veterinarians** for your horse. (Or dial "911" for the referral telephone network.)

COUNTY SHERIFF OFFICES

Apache County
370 S. Washington St.
St. Johns, AZ 85936
520-337-4321

Cochise County
836 E. Hwy. 80
Bisbee, AZ 85603
520-432-2260

Coconino County
211 N. Agassiz
Flagstaff, AZ 86001
520-774-4523

Gila County
1100 South St.
Globe, AZ 85501
520-425-4449

Graham County
523 10th Ave..
Safford, AZ 85546
520-428-3141

Greenlee County
P.O. Box 998
Clifton, AZ 85533
520-865-4149

La Paz County
1109 Arizona Ave.
Parker, AZ 85344
520-669-6141

Maricopa County
102 W. Madison St.
Phoenix, AZ 85003
602-256-1000

Mohave County
301 W. Beale St.
Kingman, AZ 86401
520-753-0753

Navajo County
P.O. Box 668
Holbrook, AZ 86025
520-524-4300

Pima County
1750 E. Benson Hwy.
Tucson, AZ 85714
520-741-4900

Pinal County
140 N. Florence St.
Florence, AZ 85232
520-868-6800

Santa Cruz County
1250 N. Hohokam Dr.
Nogales, AZ 85621
520-761-7869

Yavapai County
255 E. Gurley St.
Prescott, AZ 86301
520-771-3260

Yuma County
141 S. 3rd Ave.
Yuma, AZ 85364
520-783-4427

ARIZONA OFFICE OF TOURISM
For Arizona destination questions
1-800-842-8257

Agencies & Other Contacts

National Forest Service Offices

APACHE-SITGREAVES NATIONAL FOREST
Supervisor's Office
309 South Mountain Avenue, U.S. Hwy 180
P.O. Box 640
Springerville, AZ 85938 — 520-333-4301

Alpine Ranger District
P.O. Box 469
Alpine, AZ 85920
520-339-4384

Chevelon/Heber Ranger District
P.O. Box 968
Overgaard, AZ 85933
520-535-4481

Clifton Ranger District
Box 698
Clifton, AZ 85533
520-359-1301

Lakeside Ranger District
RR 3, Box B50
Lakeside, AZ 85929
520-368-5111

Springerville Ranger District
P.O. Box 760
Springerville, AZ 85938
520-333-4372

COCONINO NATIONAL FOREST
Supervisor's Office
2323 Greenlaw Lane
Flagstaff, AZ 86004 — 520-527-3600

Beaver Creek Ranger District
H.C. 64, Box 240
Rimrock, AZ 86335
520-567-4501

Blue Ridge Ranger District
H.C. 31, Box 300
Happy Jack, AZ 86024
520-447-2255

Long Valley Ranger District
H.C. 31, Box 68
Happy Jack, AZ 86024
520-354-2216

Mormon Lake Ranger District
4825 S. Lake Mary Road
Flagstaff, AZ 86001
520-774-1147

Peaks Ranger District
5075 N. Highway 89
Flagstaff, AZ 86004
520-526-0866

Sedona Ranger District
P.O. Box 300
Sedona, AZ 86339-0300
520-282-4119

CORONADO NATIONAL FOREST
Supervisor's Office
300 West Congress
Tucson, AZ 85701 — 520-670-4552

Douglas Ranger District
RR 1, Box 228-R
Douglas, AZ 85607
520-364-3468

Nogales Ranger District
303 Old Tucson Rd.
Nogales, AZ 85621
520-281-2296

Safford Ranger District
P.O. Box 709
Safford, AZ 85548-0709
520-428-4150

Santa Catalina Ranger District
5700 N. Sabino Canyon Road
Tucson, AZ 85750
520-749-8700

Sierra Vista Ranger District
59990 S. Hwy 92
Hereford, AZ 85615
520-378-0311

KAIBAB NATIONAL FOREST
Supervisor's Office
800 S. 6th Street
Williams, AZ 86046 — 520-635-8200

Chalender Ranger District
501 W. Bill Williams Avenue
Williams, AZ 86046
520-635-2676

North Kaibab Ranger District
P.O. Box 248
Fredonia, AZ 86022
520-643-7395

Tusayan Ranger District
P.O. Box 3088
Grand Canyon, AZ 86023
520-638-2443

Williams Ranger District
Rt. 1, Box 142
Williams, AZ 86046
520-635-2633

PRESCOTT NATIONAL FOREST
Supervisor's Office
344 South Cortez Street
Prescott, AZ 86303 — 520-771-4700

Bradshaw Ranger District
2230 E. Highway 69
Prescott, AZ 86301
520-445-7253

Chino Valley Ranger District
P.O. Box 485
735 N. Hwy 89
Chino Valley, AZ 86323
520-636-2302

Verde Ranger District
P.O. Box 670
Camp Verde, AZ 86322-0670
520-567-4121

TONTO NATIONAL FOREST
Supervisor's Office
2324 E. McDowell Road
Phoenix, AZ 85010 — 602-225-5200

Cave Creek Ranger District
P.O. Box 5068
Carefree, AZ 85377
602-488-3441

Globe Ranger District
Rt.1, Box 33
Globe, AZ 85501
520-402-6200

Mesa Ranger District
26 N. MacDonald
P.O. Box 5800
Mesa, AZ 85211-5800
602-379-6446

Payson Ranger District
1009 E. Highway 260
Payson, AZ 85541
520-474-7900

Pleasant Valley Ranger District
P.O. Box 450
Young, AZ 85554
520-462-3311

Tonto Basin Ranger District
HC 02 Box 4800
Roosevelt, AZ 85545
520-467-3200

Arizona State Parks
Main Offices
1300 West Washington St.
Phoenix, AZ 85007 — 602-542-4174

Alamo Lake State Park
Box 38
Wenden, AZ 85357
520-669-2088

Catalina State Park
Box 36986
Tucson, AZ 85740
520-628-5798

Dead Horse Ranch State Park
Box 144
Cottonwood, AZ 86326
520-634-5283

Lost Dutchman State Park
6109 N. Apache Trail
Apache Junction, AZ 85219
602-982-4485

Red Rock State Park
P.O. Box 3864
West Sedona, AZ 86340
520-282-6907

Tubac Presidio State Hist. Park
Box 1296
Tubac, AZ 85646
520-398-2252

City of Phoenix Parks, Recreation, and Library Department
Main Office
200 West Washington
Phoenix, AZ 85003 — 602-262-6861

Dreamy Draw Rec. Area
Northeast Dist. City of Phoenix
17642 N. 40th St.
Phoenix, AZ 85032
(602) 262-6696

South Mountain Park
10919 S. Central Ave.
Phoenix, AZ 85040
602-495-0222

Maricopa County Parks and Recreation
Main Office
3475 W. Durango St.
Phoenix, AZ 85009 — 602-506-2930

Adobe Dam Recreation Area
23280 N. 43rd Ave.
Glendale — 602-581-6691

Cave Creek Recreation Area
37904 N. Cave Creek Pkwy.
Cave Creek — 602-465-0431

Estrella Mtn. Regional Park
15099 W. Casey Abbott Rd. North
Goodyear — 602-932-3811

**Estrella Mtn. Regional
Park Rodeo Arena**
15099 W. Casey Abbott Rd. North
Goodyear — 602-932-3811

Lake Pleasant Regional Park
41835 N. Castle Hot Springs Rd.
Morristown — 602-780-9875

McDowell Mtn. Regional Park
15612 E. Palisades Drive
Fountain Hills — 602-471-0173

Usery Mtn. Recreation Area
3939 North Usery Pass Road
Mesa — 602-984-0032

White Tank Mtn. Reg. Park
13025 N. White Tank Mtn. Road
Litchfield Park — 602-935-2505

U. S. Dept. of the Interior Bureau of Land Management

Arizona State Office
222 N. Central
Phoenix, AZ 85004
602-417-9200

Phoenix Field Office
2015 W. Deer Valley Rd.
Phoenix, AZ 85027
602-780-8090

National Park Service
Southern Arizona Group
202 E. Earll Dr., Suite 115
Phoenix, AZ 85012 — 602-640-5250

Saguaro National Park East
3693 South Old Spanish Trail
Tucson, AZ 85730-5699
520-733-5153

Saguaro National Park West
2700 N. Kinney Road
Tucson, AZ 85743
520-733-5158

Coronado National Memorial
4101 E. Montezuma Canyon Road
Hereford, AZ 85615
520-366-5515

Other Agencies

Pima Cty. Parks & Rec. Dept.
1204 West Silverlake
Tucson, AZ 85713
520-740-2680

City of Tucson Parks Dept.
900 South Randolph
Tucson, AZ 85716
520-791-4873

Kofa National Wildlife Refuge
356 West First Street
P.O. Box 6290
Yuma, AZ 85364
520-783-7861

Equipment Check List for Trail Riders

Much of this equipment can remain in your horse trailer or vehicle, but it should all be checked periodically to make certain it is in good condition.

Some items are essential to have with you on your ride. If you plan to overnight with your horse, your list expands to include anything you would need to provide a safe trip for you and your horse.

If you plan an extended ride with a larger group of equestrians, someone in the group should assemble a set of first-aid items from the **Veterinarians' List of Medications** to have available while the group is out on the trail.

Here are the lists, glance over them every time you prepare for a trip into Arizona's vast network of fascinating trails!

Check List for your Ride

- Hoof knife (or hoof pick)
- Insect repellent (Many equestrians carry small packets of Avon Skin-So-Soft for both horse and rider)
- Pocket knife
- Comb (for removing cactus spines)
- Leather lacing (for emergency tack repairs)
- Matches or lighter
- Horseshoe replacement equipment (such as an "Easy Boot," or a set of horseshoer's tools and one front and one back shoe)
- Waterproof saddle cover (in case you must dismount in a rain/ lightning storm to walk your horse to a safer, sheltered location)
- Halter and lead rope
- Water
- Handkerchief or bandanna
- Riding gloves
- Poncho or other water repellent rain protection garment
- Rider's hat or helmet
- Trail guide and maps
- Vet Wrap, gauze, and Betadine
- Fence pliers
- Long-sleeved shirt and chaps (if riding in brushy country)
- Sunscreen
- Chapped lip medication
- Snack
- Camera
- Compass
- Flashlight
- Emergency signalling device (mirror, whistle, cellular phone, etc.)
- Hobbles (if your horse is trained to be hobbled)

Horse Trailer Check List

- Water containers for horses (5-gallon jugs work fine, or there are many other specialized, larger water tanks available for use in horse trailers). Allow for 20 gallons per horse per day.
- Water and feed buckets
- Large feeders for keeping feed off the ground, or a hay net or feed bag
- Leather punch
- Extra saddle blanket (in case one gets wet in the rain or too sweaty to use again)
- Extra stirrup
- Extra lead ropes and halter
- Grooming equipment
- Shipping boots
- Horse feed
- Extra girth/cinch and cinch leathers
- Extra reins
- Horse blanket or rain sheet for cool or rainy weather
- Fly mask
- Fly spray
- Scissors
- Rope for picket line, portable electric fence, portable corral sections, or other type of long-term tethering equipment for overnight rides
- Large flashlight or lantern

Veterinarians' List of Medications

(Medical emergency first aid kit for vehicle or trailer)

The following list was compiled by three knowledgeable veterinarians, William F. Hartnell, D.V.M. (the author's father); Vicki Baumler, D.V.M., Phoenix, (an active long-distance trail rider); and Carolyn Lee, D.V.M., Dewey (a team penning competitor). Both Dr. Baumler and Dr. Lee specialize in equine medicine. They suggest that you work with your veterinarian to make certain that you know how to recognize signs of trouble and to perform simple first aid on your horse until you can reach professional help.

These veterinarians also suggests that you purchase a stethoscope and practice listening to your horse's normal heartbeat of 38-42 beats per minute so you can tell the difference when a horse's heart rate increases. You can listen to normal intestinal noise as well, so you can detect colic conditions when they arise. (A stethoscope can be purchased for under $20 at feed or veterinary supply stores.)

These veterinarians also suggest you ask your veterinarian to show you how to take your horse's temperature if you've never done this. A human digital thermometer works well (a horse's normal temperature is between 98 and 100 degrees).

The veterinarians' list of medications and first-aid items to have on hand for emergencies includes:

- Phenylbutazone (Bute) in paste or tablet form
- Antibiotic Ophthalmic Ointment
- Oral Antibiotic Tablets (Sulfa trimethoprim keeps well for long periods)
- Saline or Clear Eyes Liquid
- Digital Thermometer
- Stethoscope
- Elasticon Tape and Sterile Pads
- Polo Wrap, Vet Wrap, and Quilts (baby disposable diapers also work well temporarily for large wounds) Have your veterinarian show you how to apply leg wraps if you've not done this before.
- Antibiotic Ointment (Furacin works well)
- Antibiotic Scrub
- Antibiotic Solution
- Banamine Paste (optional, injectable by syringe - get use and dosage information from your veterinarian)
- Acepromzine Tranquilizer (optional; injectable by syringe - get use and dosage information from your veterinarian)
- Horse Liniment, liquid
- Electrolytes (paste form in tube, or powder form) to restore salt-deprived horses after heavy sweating on long and very strenuous rides.
- Bran (mixed with water to make a mash for a horse with colic)

- ***Remember...take only pictures, and leave only hoof prints!***

Prairie Dog

Trail Manners

- Stay on the trail. Cutting new routes causes erosion.

- Although horses have the right-of-way in trail etiquette, always be ready to accommodate other trail users when common sense and safety dictate.

- Protect the trees when tying up your horse. Cushion tether ropes around trees and use tether lines between trees so horses won't damage the roots.

- Bring a rake, shovel, and container to remove manure from parking lots or other places where manure would disturb others.

- Walk around muddy areas in roads and trails where prudent.

- Many trails require dogs to be leashed at all times and some trails prohibit them entirely. Check with your Contact Agency.

- Carry a small trowel to bury human waste and toilet paper at least 4-6" deep, a minimum of 100 feet from any water and never in drainage bottoms.

- Do all washing at least 100 feet from water sources.

- Do not litter, or tie trail markers to trees. Carry out all refuse. Do not try to bury garbage, the animals will just dig it up!

Overnight Camping

- Try to camp 200 or more feet from lakes, streams, meadows, and trails when you have a choice.

- Determine if campfires are permitted. If needed, back country backpacking stoves are economical and lightweight. If you build a campfire, use an existing fire ring rather than making your own and make sure that your fire is out when you leave.

- If you are riding with pack horses or mules, select a campsite that can accommodate your animals without damage to the area. Graze animals in higher elevations on north and east slopes, leaving winter forage for wildlife on the more exposed south and west slopes.

- Use picket or hitch lines, hobbles, portable electric fences, or portable corrals to contain horses or mules. Utilize hard ground for picket line areas whenever possible. Pack in a good supply of processed feed for your horse to prevent overgrazing around the campsite. (National Park Service areas do not allow grazing of stock.)

- **If you stay more than a day or two in a campsite, move your camp at least twice daily to avoid waste accumulation, injury to plants and overgrazing.**

Trail Safety

- **Think safety and don't take any unnecessary risks! Help is often far away.**
- Be aware of the physical capabilities of yourself, your horse and your riding companions.
- Ride at a safe speed and approach each bend in the trail with caution.
- Dismount when you approach dangerous areas in the trail or turn back rather than endangering yourself or your horse.
- Protective head gear should be worn at all times.
- It is always safer to ride in a group than alone.
- Always get an extended weather report before a ride. Especially in the higher elevations, fast-moving weather fronts can become a serious hazard.
- Check with the contact agencies for valuable advice on trails, campsites, and potential problems. Most local agencies will be aware of trail changes in their jurisdiction.
- *Hypothermia* — to prevent exposure to inclement weather, always have proper clothing for yourself and blankets for your horse. Even in the summer you can be subjected to hypothermia in the higher elevations. Hypothermia is the progressive physical and mental collapse that accompanies the cooling of the inner core of the human body. Hypothermia can occur when a person is wet and cold for too long a period and is aggravated by wind and exhaustion. It is the primary killer of outdoor recreationists.

   If you think you or someone in your party is in danger of hypothermia, stop and get a fire started. Try to create cover and get that person into dry clothes and near the fire. While this is being done, someone can be prewarming a sleeping bag, either at the fire or by lying in it. Provide warm drinks. Keep warm until all symptoms disappear.
- If you are attacked by bees, get off your horse quickly, leading it away at a run and protect your eyes from stings. If you have allergic reactions to insect bites or stings be sure to always carry your prescription with you.
- Thunderstorms and their lightning are just as dangerous at the edges as in the middle. Move quickly at the first sign of such a storm. One recommended shelter is to go as deep into a grove of trees as you can get. Another is to get yourself and your horse as low to the ground as possible. The safest places for you and your horse during a lightning storm is in your vehicle or horse trailer.
- If you are in a remote area and need to signal for help, the distress signal is 3 signals with 30 second intervals. These can be visual, (mirrors, flashlights, etc.) or sound. Visual signals travel the farthest.

Hitchin' Post Restaurants

Have you ever wanted to ride up to a bar or restaurant on your horse, tie it to a hitching post and stroll in for a drink or a meal?

Most Arizona trail riders have respect and admiration for the men and women of the West who pioneered the state on horseback. Happily, there are a few places that still cater to equestrians, helping to preserve the character of Arizona's yesteryear. These places have kept a hitching post or two for horseback patrons, and encourage them to rest their legs inside while their horses rest theirs outside!

Here's a partial list of some of the special places where you'll find excellent food and drinks, meet great people and shop talk about horses to your heart's content.

Northern Arizona

Chuckwagon Steakhouse   (520) 368-5800
4040 Porter Mountain Road, Lakeside-Pinetop area
Between Show Low and Pinetop just north of State Highway 260. Turn north at mile marker 350 on Porter Mountain Road. Travel 1.5 miles to the restaurant, on the west side of the road. Family style steakhouse, dinners only. This restaurant is loaded with hitchin' posts, as it is adjacent to Porter Mountain Stables.

Hannagan's Meadow Lodge and Restaurant   (520) 339-4370
South of Alpine
South of Alpine on Highway 191, on the west side of the road. Across the road from the Hannagan Meadow Trailhead. Good menu.

Kirkland Bar & Restaurant   (520) 442-3408
Main Street, Kirkland
Located in the town of Kirkland between Kirkland Junction and Skull Valley on the way to Prescott. A favorite weekend place for the local ranchers.

Kohl's Ranch Restaurant and Bar   (520) 478-4211
East of Payson on Highway 260 near Christopher Creek.
Tie your horse to hitching posts beside the bar and under the shade trees just above sparkling Tonto Creek.

The Oxbow Saloon   (520) 474-8585
Main Street, downtown Payson
Branding irons and brands decorate this casual western bar. It is a local gathering place that turns wild during rodeo week.

Pete's Place   (520) 474-9963
Highway 260, Star Valley
East of Payson, by the roping arena on the south side of the road. Plenty of room for horse trailers. Hamburgers are the hallmark of this restaurant and bar.

Central Arizona

Buffalo Chip Saloon   (602) 488-9118

6811 E. Cave Creek Road, Carefree

An old west saloon with lots of authentic western furnishing and lots of entertainment. Western band and special events planned throughout the year. Hitching post and water trough for your horse's relaxation.

Cowboy Cafe   (520) 684-2807

4415 N. Tegner Street (Highway 89), Wickenburg

North of the stop light intersection of Highway 60 and 93, just across the bridge and on the west side of the street. There is a small hitching rail. Friendly folks and good home cookin'.

Greasewood Flat   (602) 585-9430

27000 N. Alma School Parkway, Scottsdale

Turn east off Alma School Parkway just south of Reata Pass Restaurant. This is a very rustic and very popular "hidden" outdoor bar and limited menu restaurant that is a mecca for everything from movie stars to urban cowboys to whatever. Lots of folks stop in here to just have a casual good time around the wood-burning warmers in the winter and under the shade trees in the summer. Two rows of hitching posts are located behind the bar/kitchen building. Music most evenings, open 7 days a week. There's no telephone here, but you can call for information at the number provided.

Harold's Corral   (602) 488-1906

6895 E. Cave Creek Rd., Carefree

North of Phoenix. This is a great place to stop for food or libations after riding the 7 Springs Trails. They have a wide variety of food choices and prices. There's a hitching rail and large dirt parking lot west of the restaurant.

Mammoth Steakhouse and Saloon   (602) 983-6402

4650 N. Mammoth Mine Road, Apache Junction

At Goldfield just off State Route 88 to Apache Lake, near Lost Dutchman State Park. Interesting replicas of early mining camp buildings. Large parking area for horse trailers and hitching rails down the hill and on the east side of the Steakhouse.

New River Station Cafe & Saloon   (602) 465-7920

47020 N. Black Canyon Highway, New River

North of Phoenix on the access road on the east side of Interstate 17, between Desert Hills Exit 229 and New River Exit 232. This is an old stage coach stop with a large covered patio area for private parties and special events. There is a bar and restaurant with great Mexican food. Large parking area for horse trailers.

Roadrunner Steakhouse & Saloon   (602) 465-7888

47801 N. Black Canyon Highway, Phoenix

On the freeway access road at the New River Exit 232 off Interstate 17, north of Phoenix and east of Interstate 17 at the corner of New River Road. Hitching posts, great outdoor patio area, friendly bar and a restaurant that features mesquite-grilled meals. There is a turn-around parking area and plenty of room for horse trailers.

The Stables Restaurant and Lounge   (602) 268-9462
10222 South Central Avenue, Phoenix
  In the South Mountain area. This informal bar and restaurant is beside the All Western Stables at the end of Central Avenue just before the entrance into South Mountain Park. There are hitching posts behind the restaurant.

T-Bone Steakhouse   (602) 276-0945
10037 S. 19th Avenue, Phoenix
  In the South Mountain area, south of Baseline Road. There are long hitching posts for large numbers of equestrians and a large parking lot for horse trailers. Easy access to South Mountain Park trails. Opens at 5:00 p.m. for dinner. An ideal gathering place for horseback riders.

Southern Arizona

Fred's Arena Bar and Restaurant   (520) 883-7337
9650 S. Avra Road, Tucson
  The owners of this restaurant also own horses and have plenty of room at their hitching posts! Fred's is located 20 miles west of Tucson and is reached by taking the Interstate 19 exit to Nogales off Interstate 10. Turn right at Exit 99 on Ajo Way and travel 20 miles until you reach Sierrita Mountain Road. Turn left and drive 1.25 miles to Ava Road. Left on Ava for .5 mile. Located on the corner of Ava and S. Avra Road. Top sirloin and T-Bone steaks are the favorites at this restaurant.

Lil' Abners Steak House   (520) 744-2800
8500 N. Silverbell Rd, Tucson
  Exit Interstate 10 north of Tucson on Ina Road, Exit 248, turn west and travel approximately one mile until you reach Silverbell Road. Turn north (right) on Silverbell Road for 2 miles. Hitching posts and a large parking lot for horse trailers. Favorites are 2 pound Porterhouse steaks or the ribs.

The Stage Stop Inn   (520) 394-2211
301 McKeown St., Patagonia
  Southeast of Tucson on State Route 82. In ranch country. Across from the historic Railroad Depot, downtown Patagonia. Hitching posts at the front and a long hitching rail beside the depot.

The Steak Out   (520) 455-5205
P.O. Box 99, Sonoita
  On State Highway 83, 25 miles south of Interstate 10, at the junction of the Sonoita Highway at Wentworth Road. Mesquite broiled steaks, chicken and ribs. Plenty of horse trailer parking.

Webb's Old Spanish Trail Steakhouse   (520) 885-7782
5400 South Old Spanish Trail, Tucson
  Located just past Saguaro National Monument on the east side of Tucson. They serve great baby back ribs and prime rib. This would be a super place to end a ride on the fabulous trails at Saguaro National Park East. Plenty of room for horse trailers at this restaurant.

Overnight Accommodations

The following list of boarding locations is offered as a guide and is not inclusive of all facilities available. It is important to make reservations. Telephone numbers and information were current at the time of publication, but changes must be expected.

Many of these locations provide spaces for overnight parking of campers and motor homes; others allow tenting. Some offer bed-and-breakfast or overnight lodging. The facilities not providing these accommodations are indicated with an asterisk (*).

Most of the boarding facilities listed require an up-to-date immunization record of horses to be boarded. Make a photocopy of your horse's vaccination records and carry this with your shipping papers. Some of the facilities listed will provide feed for your horse, for an extra charge. Always carry adequate feed for your horse, however, because the facility may not provide the type of feed to which your horse is accustomed.

Northern Region

*Bigman's Horseback Trail Rides　　　　　　　　　　1-800-551-4039
P. O. Box 360426
Monument Valley, UT 84536

This boarding facility is located in the Monument Valley National Park area. Facilities include corrals and water only for your horse. Bring your own feed. Call ahead for fees, directions, and reservations.

Flying Hart Barn　　　　　　　　　　　　　　　　(520) 526-2788
8400 N. Highway 89, Flagstaff
Flagstaff, AZ 86004

Exit 201 off Interstate 40 and 3.5 miles north on Highway 89. Facilities include 18 indoor stalls, 4 holding pens, hay and camper/vehicle parking. Connecting trails to Coconino National Forest wilderness areas.

Greyfire Farm Bed & Breakfast　　　　　　　　　　(520) 284-2340
1240 Jacks Canyon Road
Sedona, AZ 86351

Take Exit 298 off Interstate 17 on SR 179 to Sedona. Travel 7 miles to intersection at Jacks Canyon Road. Turn east and travel 1.6 miles. There are 2 indoor/outdoor stalls. Two-room bed and breakfast facility available by reservation. Access to trails.

*Hitchin' Post Stables, Inc.　　　　　　　　　　(520) 774-1719
448 Lake Mary Road
Flagstaff, AZ 86001

Exit 195B off Interstate 40, Lake Mary Road. Facilities include 19 indoor stalls, large arena. Access to Coconino National Forest trails and the Arizona Trail.

Houston Mesa Horse Camp
Payson, Arizona　　　　　　　　　　　　　　　　1-800-280 CAMP

Located approximately one mile north of Payson on State Highway 87. Turn east on Houston Mesa Road, Forest Route 199, 0.1 mile. Horse Camp is on right (south) side of Houston Mesa Road. An outstanding, well-designed overnight/weekly camping facility for equestrians. 31 camp sites with either pull-through or back-in parking with ample room for a horse trailer, truck/camper, or motor home. Two large group campsites also available (room for 75-100 campers with horses). Each campsite has two pipe corrals, a picket line, picnic table, barbecue grill, and shade trees. Water spigots in numerous locations. Horse watering troughs. The campground has running water, flush toilets, wash basins (cold water only), in four large restroom facilities. Showers, water hoses, and dump station available in adjacent non-equestrian campground. Just a few miles from the Payson Rodeo Grounds, and 12 area equestrian trailheads are within 30 minutes driving time. Reservations should be made in advance through U.S. Forest Service by writing USFS National Recreation Reservations, P.O. Box 900, Cumberland, Maryland 21501-0900, or by calling 1-800-280-2267.

Juniper Well Ranch Bed & Breakfast   (520) 442-3415
P. O. Box 10623
Prescott, AZ 86034
      West of Prescott 8.2 miles on Iron Springs Road. North on Contreras Road (102A or FR 336) after mile 8 marker. Go 4 miles to the end of Contreras Road at its junction with Tonto Road. Turn right on Tonto Road, go 150 yards, and turn right at the sign "Bonham." Two attractive log cabins furnished with country antiques and an outdoor jacuzzi. The second cabin sleeps 4. Electric fences.

L Bell Ranch
P. O. Box 65
Skull Valley, AZ 86338   (520) 442-3838
      This charming horse-boarding facility also offers a two-story ranch house. Travel 23 miles west of Prescott on Iron Springs Road, turn west at the L Bell Ranch sign and drive 5 miles on a well-maintained dirt road to the ranch. Access to Prescott National Forest.

*MCS Stables   (520) 774-5835
HC 30, Box 16
Flagstaff, AZ 86001
      Exit 337 off Interstate 17 and 2 miles south on Highway 89A to Sedona. Facilities include 8 indoor stalls with outdoor runs, 18 pipe enclosed pens, alfalfa and grain. Connects to Coconino National Forest trails. Motels within 3 miles. Excellent, well-managed facility.

Oasis Ranch   (520) 442-9559
P.O. Box 256
Skull Valley, AZ 86338
      Located 3/4 mile south of Skull Valley. From Phoenix take Highway 60 to Wickenburg, then turn north on Highway 93 for 4 miles. Turn right on Highway 89 to Congress and Yarnell, and 4 miles north of Peeples Valley turn left on County Road 15 to Kirkland. At Kirkland turn right at the stop sign, travel 3 miles and turn right on Valley Connector Road, travel one mile to lane lined with cottonwood trees. Turn left at the lane and travel past other houses to the very end. There is a small cement-bottom creek crossing just before the ranch. Two guest houses, adults only, two 12 x 24 pipe corrals with shade for guests' horses, a barn with four stalls and 12 x 20 turnouts. Very special and relaxing accommodations. Featured in *Arizona Highways* magazine.

The Opal Ranch Inn Bed and Breakfast   (520) 472-6193
2160 Moonlight Drive
HC4, Box 29
Payson, AZ 85541
East of Payson in Star Valley, 2 1/2 miles south of Highway 260. Turn south at Pete's Place Restaurant, just after Lamplighter RV Park, on Moonlight Drive. First 1 1/2 miles paved, last mile all-weather road. Two pipe corrals, four stalls in barn, 3-acre pature. 3 guest rooms (adults only) with truly wonderful country breakfasts, homemade jams and jellies and farm fresh eggs. Open year round. Trails into Tonto National Forest from ranch.

Pinetop Equestrian Center
P. O. Box 1183
Pinetop, AZ 85935   (520) 369-1000
Located on State Highway 260 between Show Low and Springerville at mile marker 355. Enter Pinetop Country Club and travel 1.4 miles on Buck Springs Road. Camping area, corrals, stalls, and picket lines, restrooms, and pull-through spaces for 15 horse trailers. Round pen and arena. Access to the White Mountain Trail System.

*Porter Mountain Stables
4040 Porter Mountain Road
Lakeside, AZ 85929   (520) 368-5306
Located just north of State Highway 260 in Pinetop-Lakeside, between Show Low and Springerville. Turn north from State Highway 260 on Porter Mountain Road at mile marker 350.1. Travel 1.5 miles to stables, on the west side of the road. Open from Memorial Day to Labor Day. Access to White Mountain Trail System.

Prescott Ranch
25755 N. Old Hwy. 89   (520) 636-9737 or (800) 684-7433
P.O. Box 579
Paulden, AZ 86334
Located approximately 30 minutes north of Prescott on Highway 89 to Chino Valley. Pass through Chino Valley and Paulden, turn east near mile marker 339, to Old Highway 89, following the road another 200 yards to the gate on the right. Inside and outside stalls with 12 x 24 runs. Trail ride groups welcome. Trails into Prescott National Forest from ranch.

Snowy Mountain Inn   (520) 735-7576
P.O. Box 337
Greer, AZ 85927
Located 31 miles east of Pinetop-Lakeside approximately 1 1/2 miles south of Highway 260 on Highway 373, on east (left) side of road. Four cabins with 12 x 24 pens. Near Greer area lakes and streams for trout fishing, signed riding trails and cross country ski trails in Apache-Sitgreaves National Forest and Mt. Baldy.

Toltec Horse Motel   (520) 289-5631
P. O. Box 723
Winslow, AZ 86047
Exit 252 off Interstate 40 east of Flagstaff just outside of Winslow. Turn north after exiting Interstate 40, then turn west on the frontage road. Travel approximately .5 mile

and turn right on Painted Desert Drive. Turn right again on the driveway to the Toltec Horse Motel barn area. Six large pens with shade covers and four box stalls available. Call ahead for information and reservations. Hay available for purchase. Limited space available to park self-contained campers or motor homes for overnight stay.

Central Region

Desert Retreat Ranch
Florence, AZ   (602) 983-1122
Mailing Address:
P.O. Box 1933
Apache Junction, AZ 85217
  Located just north of Florence and south of the Gila River bridge on Highway 79. Turn east on Diversion Dam Road and travel approximately 7 miles to a steel bridge. Cross the bridge and follow the short road ending at the ranch house. RV hookups, 14 horse pens, 100 x 200 arena, 50 ft. round pen, large pasture, showers, bathrooms, swimming pool. Near Box Canyon and the Arizona Trail in White Canyon Wilderness area.

Horsepitality R.V. Park
Highways 93, 60, and 89
Wickenburg, AZ 85358   (520) 684-2519
  Located 2 miles south of Wickenburg on Highways 93, 60, and 89, on west side of the road. Facilities include 20 pipe corrals, large arena, and very large RV parking area.

Indian Springs Ranch Bed & Breakfast
13131 W. Indian Springs Rd.
Goodyear, AZ 85338   (602) 932-2076
Southwest of Phoenix on Interstate 10, 15 miles. Take Exit 131 south to Phoenix International Raceway, then travel 2 more miles west to ranch sign. Horse corral. Forty acre 1974 Spanish hacienda with Spanish furnishings.

J Bar J Ranch
P.O. Box 524
Wickenburg, AZ 85358   (520) 684-9142 or (800) 537-2173
  Located 1 1/2 miles north of Wickenburg on Highway 93. Turn right at mile marker 198 on Rincon Road. Travel 2 miles to ranch entrance. Five guest rooms, southwest decor. Outdoor patio area, reading room, wet bar. 2 outdoor pens with shade for guests' horses. Health validation required.

Stage Line Ranch
102 W. Desert Hills Dr.
Phoenix, AZ 85027   (602) 465-7492
  Located north of Carefree Highway and 1/4 mile east of 7th Street on Desert Hills Drive, on north side of road just past the fire station. Facilities include 8 indoor stalls, 25 outdoor pens, 2 holding pens, large lighted arena. Hay available. Trailer parking, one camper hookup, and 2 bedroom Bed and Breakfast ranch house available with reservations. Ownership, negative Coggins, and health validation required.

Southern Region

Apache Springs Guest Ranch
P.O. Box 230
Sonoita, AZ 85637 (520) 455-5232
 Located in the heart of ranching country 4.5 miles north of Sonoita, 5 miles west of Highway 83 on Gardner Canyon Road. Follow signs to Gardner Canyon trailhead. Take the left fork into the ranch just before the trailhead and follow the Apache Springs Ranch signs. Large RV and tent camping area, no RV hookups for groups. Spacious lawns, BBQ building, a beautifully furnished casita for overnight guests. Barns with stalls, covered arena. Former Arabian horse facility with ample amenities. Located on the route of the Arizona Trail. Call for reservations. Large groups welcome.

Cactus Country RV Resort
10195 S. Houghton Road
Tucson, AZ 85747 1-800-777-8799
 Take Exit 275 off Interstate 10 east of Tucson. Travel 0.25 miles north on Houghton Road. One very large holding pen and full camper hookups.

Muleshoe Ranch Preserve
RR 1, Box 1542
Willcox, AZ 85643 (520) 586-7072
 Campgrounds and 5 cottages . There are 3 large wooden corrals for guests' horses (no charge). Water is provided, but no feed. Call for directions, road conditions and information. This facility is very remote. It is managed by the Nature Conservancy.

Rocking M Ranch Bed and Breakfast
6265 N. Camino Verde
Tucson, AZ 85743 1-888-588-2457, (520) 744-2457 or FAX (520) 744-0824
Located northwest of Tucson. Take exit 248 and go west on Ina Road 2 miles. Turn south on Camino Verde, travel 1.5 miles to end of road. Entrance is on right hand side.

Sunglow Guest Ranch
Turkey Creek Road
HCR 1, Box 385
Pearce, AZ 85625 (520) 824-3334
 Located in the foothills on the eastern slopes of the Chiricahua Mountains south of Willcox and Interstate 10, one hour east of Tucson. Guest ranch with 15 casitas, most with kitchenettes, or full board also available. Quiet retreat. 10 pipe horse corrals for guests. Trails into Chiricahua Mountains are in the pines, oak, juniper elevations. Old West historic area. Very well-managed facility.

Wild Horse Ranch Resort
6801 N. Camino Verde
Tucson, AZ 85743 (520) 744-1012 or FAX (520) 579-3991
 Located northwest of Tucson very near Saguaro National Park West. Take Ina Road Exit 248 off Interstate 10 north of Tucson. Travel 2.1 miles west on Ina Road. Turn south on Camino Verde 0.2 mile to ranch entrance. 28 guest rooms, 6-10 stalls available. Horse trailer parking. Negative Coggins, health, and ownership papers required.

About the Author

Jan Hancock is a member of the Arizona State Committee on Trails Board of Directors and an avid horsewoman who is active in riding groups such as the Wickenburg Las Damas organization, the Arizona State Horsemen's Association, and a number of trail riding clubs throughout the state.

Jan's interest in horses began at the age of three when her father, a veterinarian, brought two ponies to their home in the Ohio countryside. She has been riding in horse shows, rodeos, parades and for pleasure since that time. Jan has been researching and recording some of Arizona's outstanding trails for the past several years for this publication of *Horse Trails in Arizona.*

Jan is a college instructor, an artist, a world traveler and a successful sales and marketing manager in the office furnishings industry. She moved to Arizona in 1955 and resides in Phoenix.

Jan is a feature writer in state and national publications, and is listed in the top 100 *Today's Arizona Woman Business Directory.*

Jan has a strong interest in early Arizona explorers and trailblazers. She is a member of the Arizona State Parks Historic Trails Committee, a volunteer group involved in the restoration and nomination of trails for historic preservation and public recreational use. Jan is also active as a member of the Board of Directors for The Arizona Trail Association, the non-profit organization developing the trans-Arizona trail which extends from Mexico to Utah.

Partial proceeds from the sale of this book are donated by the author to trail development and preservation programs in Arizona.

Jan is currently working on a guide book on the new Arizona Trail that is scheduled to be published by Golden West Publishers in 1999-2000.

ORDER BLANK

GOLDEN WEST PUBLISHERS

☼ 4113 N. Longview Ave. • Phoenix, AZ 85014

602-265-4392 • **1-800-658-5830** • FAX 602-279-6901

Qty	Title	Price	Amount
	Arizona Cook Book	5.95	
	Arizona Outdoor Guide	6.95	
	Arizona Trivia	8.95	
	Best Barbecue Recipes	5.95	
	Chili Lovers Cook Book	5.95	
	Cowboy Cartoon Cook Book	5.95	
	Cowboy Slang	5.95	
	Discover Arizona!	6.95	
	Explore Arizona!	6.95	
	Fishing Arizona	7.95	
	Ghost Towns in Arizona	6.95	
	Hiking Arizona	6.95	
	Horse Trails in Arizona	12.95	
	Motorcycle Arizona	9.95	
	Prehistoric Arizona	5.00	
	Quick-n-Easy Mexican Recipes	5.95	
	Salsa Lovers Cook Book	5.95	
	Scorpions & other Venomous Insects/SW	9.95	
	Snakes & other Reptiles of the SW	9.95	
	Verde River Recreation Guide	9.95	

Shipping & Handling Add ⮕	U.S. & Canada Other countries	$3.00 $5.00	

☐ My Check or Money Order Enclosed $

☐ MasterCard   ☐ VISA ($20 credit card minimum)

(Payable in U.S. funds)

Acct. No.	Exp. Date
Signature	
Name	Telephone
Address	
City/State/Zip 1/98	**Call for FREE catalog** AZ Horse Trails